Cycle Repair and Maintenance

Cycle Repair and Maintenance

by A.J.Budrys
edited by Ken Evans and Allan Scott

Photography by Allan Scott

Adam and Charles Black
London

Cycle Repair and Maintenance is based on *Bicycles: How They Work and How to Fix Them* by A. J. Budrys, originally published in the USA, and adapted for the UK by Ken Evans and Allan Scott

Original text copyright © 1976 The Unifont Company
This adaptation copyright © 1984 The Unifont Company, Ken Evans and Allan Scott

First UK edition 1984

Budrys, A.J.
    Cycle repair and maintenance.
    1. Bicycles—Maintenance and repair
    I. Title   II. Scott, Allan J.J.
    III. Evans, Ken, 19— —   — — —
    629.28'772   TL430

    ISBN 0-7136-2450-7
    ISBN 0-7136-2451-5 Pbk

Published by
A & C Black (Publishers) Limited
35 Bedford Row, London, WC1R 4JH

Design and illustrations: Giolitto, Wrigley & Couch Design Partnership

Photographic credits

The publishers wish gratefully to acknowledge permission to reproduce the photographs listed above. All other photographs are by Allan Scott.

Typeset by Armitage Typo/Graphics Ltd, Huddersfield

Printed and bound in Great Britain by R. J. Acford, Chichester

Contents

Introduction

This guide illustrates and explains the systems and parts used by popular types of bicycle. It discusses how they work, suggests where they might go wrong and shows, step by step, how to go about dealing with the problems that do arise.

In that sense, the book is a repair manual. A glance at the contents page will show you the chapter you need. Within the chapter you will find diagrams, photographs and text that together should help you deal with specific problems. The facts are accurate. The photographs and diagrams have been designed to be useful even to professional mechanics. So the book should be ideal for cycling enthusiasts working at home with ordinary tools.

But the book is intended as something more than a work of reference for a cyclist with an immediate problem. If you have little detailed mechanical knowledge, it may be worth your while to read the book from cover to cover before any problems arise. It will then be that much easier to spot a problem, and you will be that much better prepared to deal with anything that does go wrong.

An understanding of how your bicycle works should also help you to avoid bad riding practices, and to show the value of regular routine maintenance. A few simple checks can prevent, or at least minimise, the risk of any major mechanical failure.

Starting with the basics

The early sections of this book deal with the simplest aspects of cycle repair and maintenance, moving on to increasingly sophisticated repairs, and eventually dealing with such complex topics as the inner workings of the freewheel block. Dealing with systems like this requires time — and patience!

The progression serves several purposes. To begin with, it arranges the repairs in ascending order of difficulty. It also allows you to gain experience — probably your most useful tool. Your skill in rebuilding a hub will largely depend on your earlier experiences with the similar but slightly less crucial bearing adjustments on front fork head races, for instance. If you are a complete novice, it will be best to familiarise yourself completely with one chapter before moving on to the next. The text will be easier to follow, and the photographs and diagrams will be easier to understand.

A second repair is always a little easier than the first — and that is the secret behind the poise, skill and dexterity of the professional mechanic.

Mistakes lead to skill

After years of coping with the full range of problems that beset mechanical systems, the professional mechanic learns all the tricks of the trade — the tricks that make one hub rebuild faster and more entertaining, though not necessarily better, than another. The professional rarely fumbles for tools — the ones he needs most often are arranged readily to hand. He rarely drops a raceful of ball bearings — he knows that if the frame is held at a particular angle the bearings will not fall out, and he knows how to hold the cup after he has removed it, while he is undoing the bearing set. But his skill is based on errors he has made in the past, probably in the privacy of his own home — and that is where you will learn the same skills.

By itself, this book is not necessarily going to turn you into a deft professional; but it will help you teach yourself as you build up your own experience. It may not be an expensive home study course, with a tempting certificate waiting to reward your efforts, but in practical terms the effect should be much the same. As your experience grows, even if some of it is only a theoretical understanding of this book, the later chapters will seem less and less forbidding. Eventually even the freewheel block will hold few terrors. Once it has actually been taken apart, any mechanism will prove less complex than a diagram would lead you to believe. Hands-on experience is worth far more than any amount of theoretical knowledge. One day you will cope successfully with a problem that would once have driven you cap in hand to the nearest cycle shop, and you will finish up with a perfectly functioning machine.

That could be a particularly rewarding and enjoyable ride.

How a bicycle works

The mechanical systems of a bicycle depend on a few basic principles, which are applied in a few generally similar ways.

To roll along as efficiently as possible, a bicycle uses a number of precision bearings, usually hard steel balls turning in adjustable cup-and-cone 'races'. These bearings are fitted where a rotating part has to bear the weight of machine and rider, or where force may be applied unevenly, as it is at the pedals and to some extent at the rear sprocket. Many of these assemblies will seem familiar to those with a little do-it-yourself experience. But even if you have some mechanical experience already, as a newcomer to bicycles you will be struck by the prevalence of tension mechanics.

Most bicycles are festooned with lever-operated cables, and each of these cables has a spring at one end. It may be a visible part of a brake or derailleur, or it may be hidden in a hub, but almost all those parts of the machine not concerned with rolling will operate on the same principle. A movable part is held in place by a spring, and pulled into a different alignment by the cable. When the cable relaxes, the spring returns the part to its original position.

One major cause of problems is slack in the cables, either because one end has come loose or because the cable has been stretched by normal use or by an accident. Another danger is a control that manages to pull too hard and too far. The diagrams show some of the ways in which this is provided for. At one end, the cable is fitted with a moulded-on ball or drum that anchors snugly into the control. At the other end a clamp is fitted, allowing the cable to be adjusted to its optimum length. But if the cable slips loose, or is pulled too far, the device it operates — a gear-changing mechanism, for instance — might fail to work, or be damaged. This could be dangerous: gear-changing needs to be precise. It could also be expensive. So derailleurs, for

1

instance, have limit stops — features that prevent the control arm from swinging too far. Because sprocket sizes vary, and their spacing can vary from one machine to another, the stops need to be adjustable. This means that even an essentially simple mechanism can appear complex to the inexperienced eye.

Again, it is hardly practicable to move clamps every time a cable stretches. So brake-cable sheaths (to choose the most obvious example) end with an adjuster threaded through a bracket. Screwing back the adjuster will lengthen the sheath, taking up the slack in the cable. A lock-nut is threaded onto the adjuster, and once the brake is correctly set the adjuster can be secured by screwing the lock-nut down tightly against the bracket. The use of lock-nuts, which force two parts tightly against each other to hold a precise adjustment, is another common feature of bicycle engineering.

Useful tools

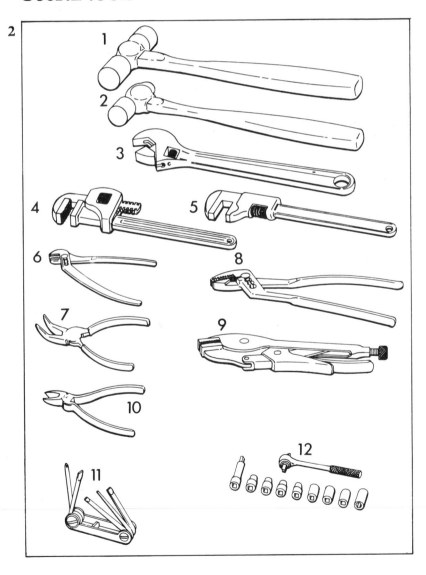

2: Common household tools can be used for many cycle repairs. You will need a hammer (1) with one rubber and one plastic head, as well as an ordinary hammer (2), an adjustable spanner (3) and pipe wrenches (4, 5) for gripping knurled fittings. Pliers (6-8) are useful, especially needle-nosed offset pliers (7), and a mole wrench (9) is always handy. Good wire-cutters (10) are essential for most bicycles. A good penknife (11) will almost certainly have some useful attachments, while a set of ¼ in socket spanners in small metric sizes is a worthwhile luxury. Try to buy tools that are light and compact, so you can carry them with you when you ride.

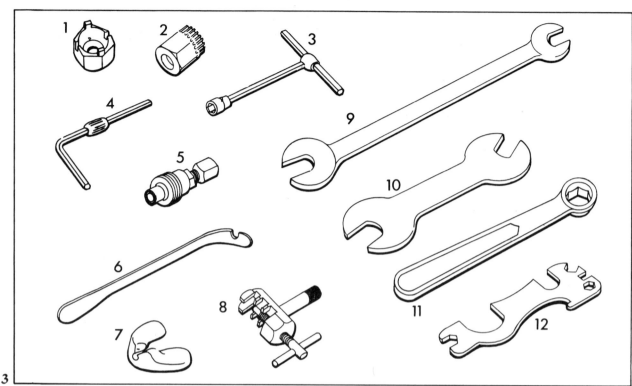

3

3: Most special tools are needed only for special jobs, but some are extremely useful. Freewheel extractors (1, 2) are for derailleur machines only, and must fit your particular model of freewheel. T- and L-spanners (3, 4) fit derailleurs and some chainwheels. The crank extractor (5) is for cotterless cranks only. The tyre lever (6), which is notched to hook onto spokes, will fit any conventional wheel. The spoke key (7) must fit the spoke nipples. The thumbscrew tool (8) is a chain-rivet extractor for opening and closing derailleur chain links. The long pedal spanner (9) and the thin cone spanner (10) are useful; the axle end-bolt spanner (11) is essential for dismantling cotterless cranksets. However, even the lowly giveaway stamped multispanner (12), with its lock-ring spanner hook and its broad U-shaped cup spanner, can often save the day.

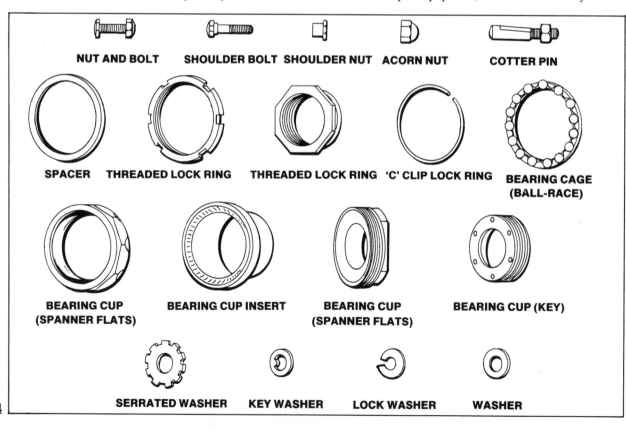

NUT AND BOLT   SHOULDER BOLT   SHOULDER NUT   ACORN NUT   COTTER PIN

SPACER   THREADED LOCK RING   THREADED LOCK RING   'C' CLIP LOCK RING   BEARING CAGE (BALL-RACE)

BEARING CUP (SPANNER FLATS)   BEARING CUP INSERT   BEARING CUP (SPANNER FLATS)   BEARING CUP (KEY)

SERRATED WASHER   KEY WASHER   LOCK WASHER   WASHER

4

Forks, frames, handlebars, saddles

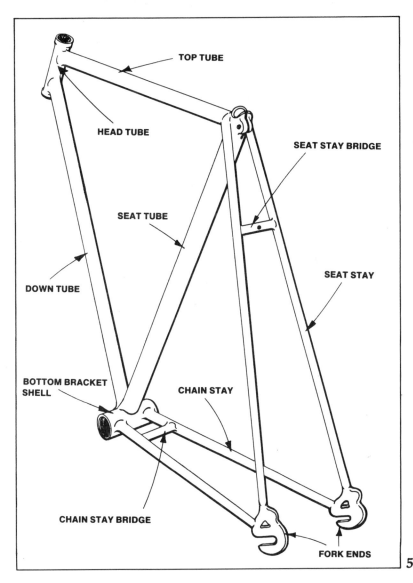

TOP TUBE

HEAD TUBE

SEAT STAY BRIDGE

SEAT TUBE

SEAT STAY

DOWN TUBE

BOTTOM BRACKET SHELL

CHAIN STAY

CHAIN STAY BRIDGE

FORK ENDS

5

5: The frame is the irreducible minimum; in theory, at least, everything else can be repaired at home. Most frames are made of thin-walled steel tubing. Some are welded; others are fitted together into lugs, and then reinforced by *brazing* (soldering with brass). The lighter and more expensive the frame, the more advisable it is to take it to a good shop if it needs straightening, or if the fork-ends are out of alignment. This particular frame has a threaded bottom bracket shell for a three-piece crankset (see page 45).

Front forks

When people talk about the 'forks' of a bicycle they invariably mean the front forks. This is the part that usually gets the blame if the machine will not follow a straight-line path as you cycle down the road.

Quite often it *is* the villain, though a front-end collision that causes visible distortion will probably also affect the angles of the head tube, the top and down tubes, and the fork column concealed inside the head tube.

In many cases the fork blades and column can be retrued by a shop equipped with the necessary jigs and tools to do so accurately. But if a fork has not been damaged in an accident, yet feels stiff or 'wobbly' when the handlebars

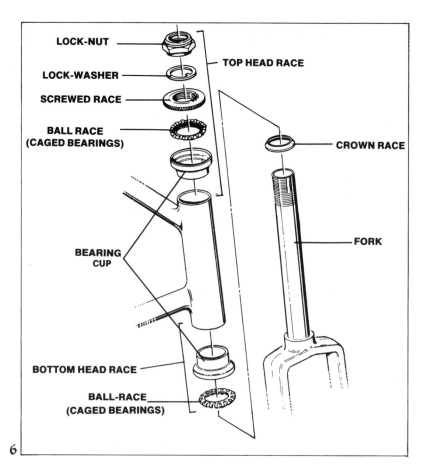

LOCK-NUT

LOCK-WASHER

SCREWED RACE

BALL RACE (CAGED BEARINGS)

TOP HEAD RACE

CROWN RACE

FORK

BEARING CUP

BOTTOM HEAD RACE

BALL-RACE (CAGED BEARINGS)

6

are turned, then the problem probably lies in the bearings — the headset.

Ultimately, the full weight carried by the front wheel rests on the crown race. Fig. 6 shows how the crown race slips over the fork column. Next come the lower bearings: these may be loose, or they may be held in a retainer or 'cage' as they nestle into the bearing cup of the bottom head race. The rolling of the balls allows the forks to turn despite the potential friction of the weight on the forks.

The upper bearings (in the top head race) provide another point of support for the fork column. This stops it wobbling. It is also the logical place for the adjuster, and the lock-nut designed to hold the adjustment.

The system works more by machining than by lubrication: the metal surfaces are curved, ground and polished until they fit together almost perfectly. A fraction of a turn of the screwed race threaded over the fork column will pull everything together into a smoothly functioning unit. The lock-washer, held in alignment by its notch or flat in the column threads, will allow the lock-nut to be tightened without disturbing the adjustment of the screwed race — particularly if the screwed race is also held motionless with a suitable tool. If these adjustments are made correctly, the forks will function reliably for a long time.

Common problems in this area usually turn out to be problems of adjustment. The screwed race may have managed to turn anticlockwise, loosening until the fork column is free to wobble. A loose lock-nut often causes this problem; it may have been badly fastened to begin with, or badly refastened after an adjustment of the handlebar stem. Nothing in the headset has anything to do with the handlebar stem, but the handlebar stem is wedged inside the fork column, and it passes through the lock-nut.

On some machines with centre-pull brakes a hanger like the one in fig. 1 is fixed between the head race and the lock-nut. Fiddling with this may sometimes loosen the lock-nut or tighten the screwed race.

Forks that have been too tight, or too loose, for any length of time cannot reliably be repaired by a simple adjustment. All parts of the headset must be inspected, and some will have to be replaced if you expect to ride the bicycle very much in the future. This is because of the structure of the cup, balls and cone — the screwed race and crown race (see fig. 6). A glance at fig. 26 may give you a clearer idea of how bearing parts are assembled.

As you can see, the balls, whether they are free or loosely held in a retainer cage, fit the full curve of the bearing cup. A cone, approaching from the other side, presents less of a curved section. Both curves fit the ball closely, but the more open cone leaves room for the lubricant. This is not needed to 'make things slippery' so much as to cool the metal of the parts.

When the adjustment of the bearing is too tight, heat from friction will exceed the cooling capacity of the lubricant, and the metal of the ball will gradually disintegrate. At first it will become pitted and cratered, like a miniature moon landscape. Then it will start to break up. All this time, its sharp-edged fragments will be tearing at the cup and the cone.

If the adjustment is too loose, the ball will rock between cup and cone, breaking down the edge of the cone curve and pounding irregular grooves, like worm trails, through the surface of the cup. At the same time the ball will develop flat spots and tear up its retainer.

As the battered bearing loses its proper shape, it cracks open. Grit enters. And that finishes the job — the entire bearing is now just so much scrap metal.

Fortunately spare parts are plentiful and cheap, and bearing sets are designed to be easily removed and rebuilt. Although few people take advantage of the fact, it is perfectly possible to rebuild a bicycle so it runs like new as long as the frame is true.

How to do it

If you are working on the front forks then the traditional position, with the machine inverted and standing on its handlebars, is obviously useless. But it is far easier to work on a frame that is not resting on the floor. The answer is to remove the wheels and hang the frame by ropes from a beam. Alternatively, you can hang the frame over the corner of a workbench, preventing it from slipping off with a piece of wood clamped across the corner of the bench. Anything will do, as long as it will hold the machine waist-high, yet allow you to lift off the frame and turn it upside down with as little trouble as possible. A broom handle over the backs of two chairs will do, but if you feel you will often be doing this kind of work, then the professional bicycle stand shown in the photographs might be a worthwhile investment.

Lay out the parts you have removed in a row, in the right order — make sure you have a jam-jar lid or something similar to hold small parts such as ball bearings. If you don't know for certain, always assume that a bearing uses loose balls, and be ready to catch them.

Take worn parts to the shop with you, and take the forks as well. Make quite sure that any replacements you buy are the right type and the right size — check by threading the new part onto the fork column in the shop. Never force a threaded part — the metal of the fork column is soft, and the threads can easily be stripped in this way.

If you are dealing with loose balls, count them. If you lose count, buy enough replacements to encircle the cup completely, then take one away. Make sure, if you can, that the replacement balls are exactly the same size as the original ones. If they do turn out to be slightly larger, or slightly smaller, make sure that all the balls you *use* are the same size.

A cup or a ball may look acceptable — don't assume that it will always have to be replaced. Any cup that has been used is going to show a brighter streak in the metal; if the streak is of uniform width, and does not look like a groove, then the cup is probably worth keeping. But in most cases a ball that has been running for a year or so should probably be replaced even if it looks round and smooth. Bearings are vital to the performance of the machine — if in doubt, throw it out.

Use the best lubricant you can find — we recommend white molybdenum grease. Put enough in the cup that the balls still show when you insert them but will not fall out when the cup is turned upside down. Put a little on the cone, too. That's enough. Now close the bearing and tighten it until it feels silky and positive when you turn it in your hand.

Keeping things clean is important. As you take the bearing apart, wipe each part clean with a soft cloth before using a tool on it. Then wash the parts. When you reassemble them, make sure that all the parts are spotless apart from lubricant. You can use detergent and water for cleaning provided that you rinse and dry the parts immediately. Solvents are useful, but many are very poisonous and may easily catch fire. Believe everything you have heard about them — and more. Make sure you work with constant ventilation, keep solvent containers closed, and *never* leave soaked rags lying about. Don't be too afraid of solvents, but do make sure you respect them. You will not regret it.

7: After removing the handlebars and stem as a unit (see fig. 15) you will come to the lock-nut. The washer underneath it will have a lug or a flat spot corresponding to a notch or flat spot on the fork column. The washer is a snug fit, and must be removed straight up — a thin-bladed screwdriver can often be helpful here. Now loosen, but do not remove, the adjuster. If it is knurled rather than flatted or keyed, wrap it with thin cloth and undo it with an adjustable spanner or pipe wrench.

8: Now invert the frame. Finish removing the adjuster by hand — be ready to catch the bearings or the retainer. Remember that the fork is now completely free; if it uses loose balls, the bottom set may fall out as well if you accidentally bump the fork. Some of the balls could fall into the frame tubing, and might even get into the bottom bracket.

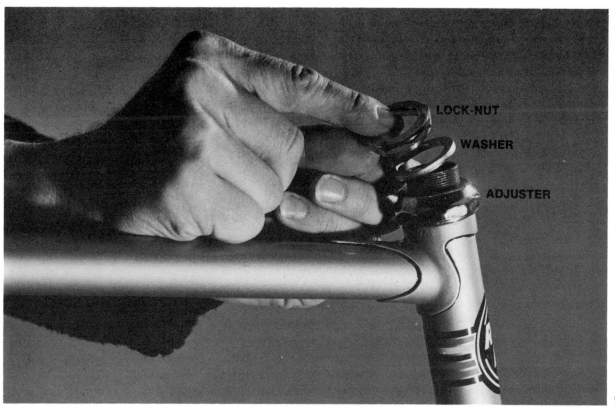

7

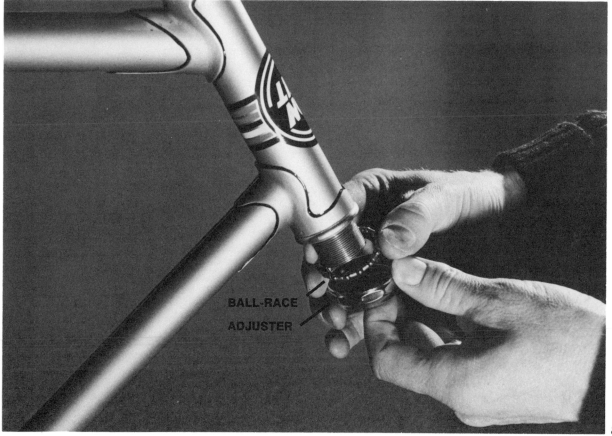

8

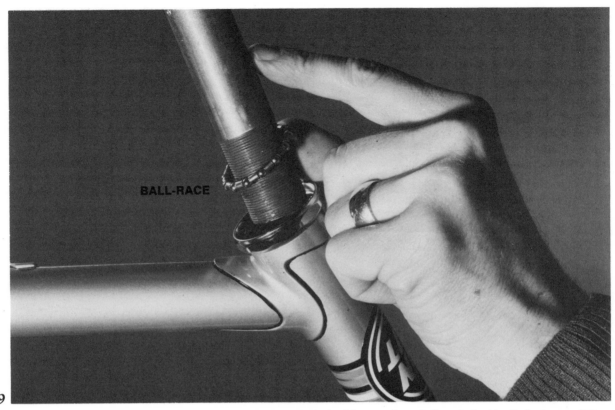

9: Now lift out the fork. If there are loose balls to deal with, tilt the frame a little to make sure they drop straight out through the head tube.

10: The bearing cups can be punched out with a dowel and a soft-headed hammer if they need to be replaced. The crown race, too, is only pressed on, but it is a very snug fit. However, it should yield to blunt punches with any hard metal rod and a hard hammer. To replace the bearing cups, use a soft hammer or a wooden mallet. If you are hammering at one end of a frame, do check that another end is not being crushed against something, and make sure there is nothing trapped under the frame that might be damaged by the force of the blows.

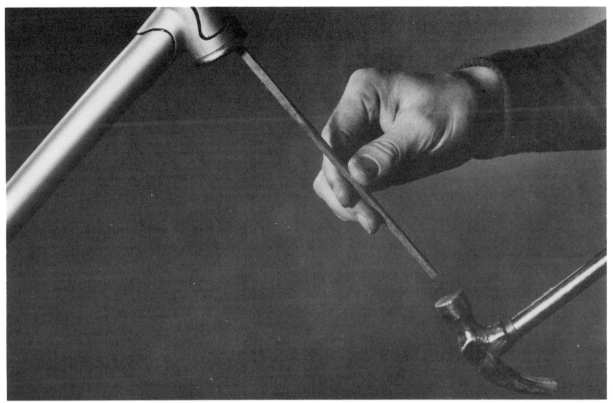

10A

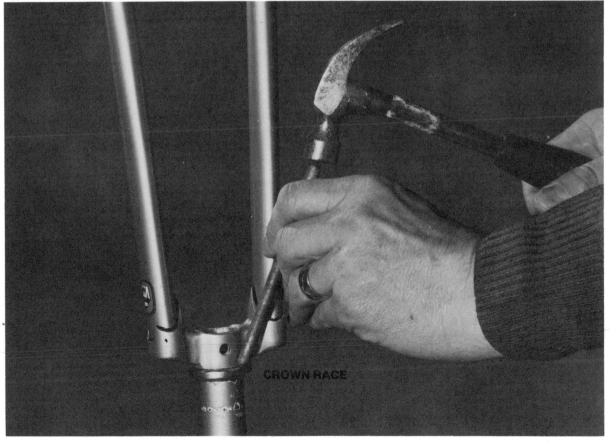

CROWN RACE

10B

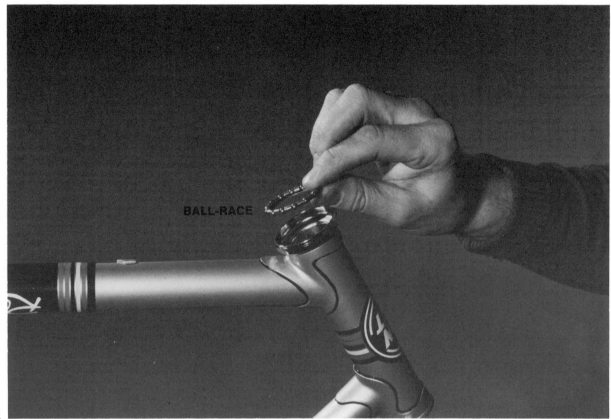

11

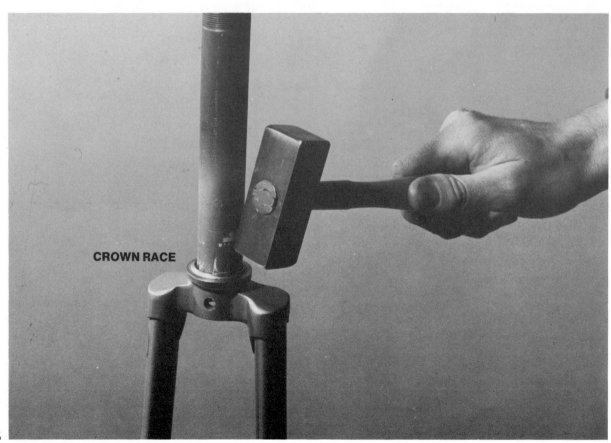

12

11: Now insert the balls of the bottom head bearing. Ball-races generally dish into the cup; if the race itself is cup-shaped rather than symmetrical, then it nests.

12: Putting back the crown race is a particularly delicate job. Misplaced blows can scar the tube threads, chip paint at the fork crown, or damage the race or the crown seat on which it rests. A touch of grease should help.

13: Now put everything else back together in the right order.

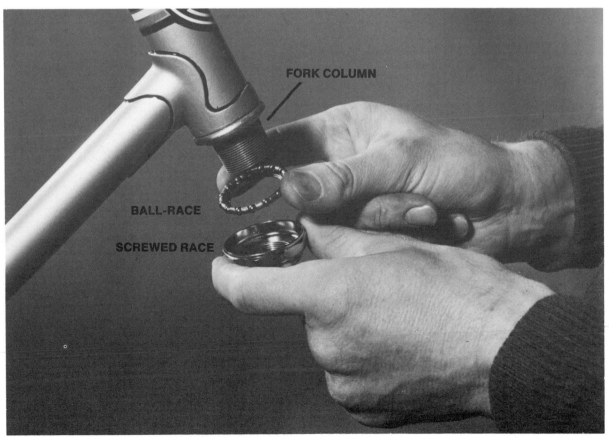

FORK COLUMN

BALL-RACE

SCREWED RACE

13A

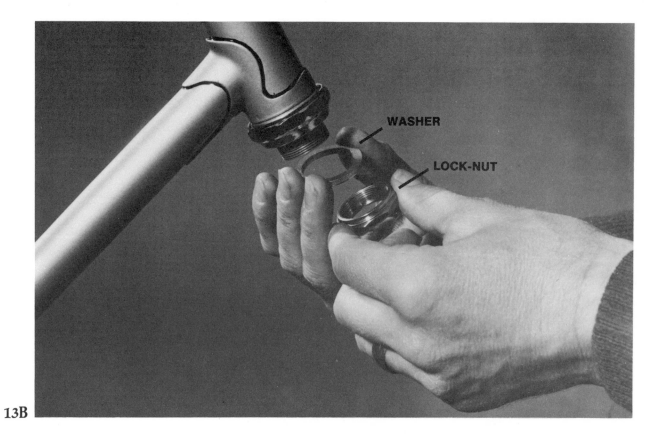

13B

14: Adjust the race by hand, then tighten the lock-nut against it. It usually helps to hold the adjuster with a tool, or at least, as here, with your other hand. See page 13 for the correct adjustment.

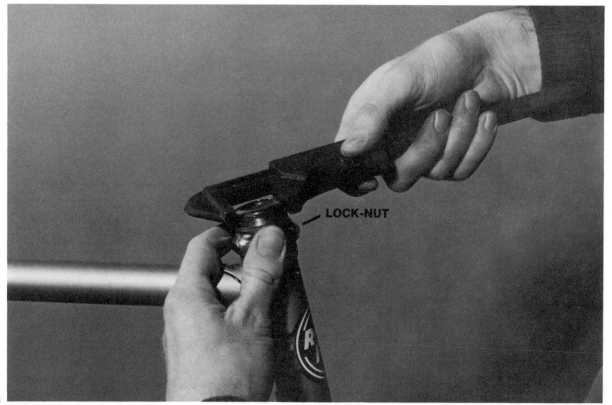

14

Stems

Handlebar stems come in a wide variety of types and lengths. There are various ways to install them, but for all practical purposes we can say that they always slip into the tube of the fork column, and are wedged there by tightening an expander bolt whose head protrudes from the top of the stem. The head will either carry flats for tightening with a spanner, or a socket for an Allen key.

The long expander bolt is threaded through a wedge at the bottom of the handlebar stem. This wedge may be a conical plug, and the plug may have a lug that fits into a slot cut part way up the stem. Once the stem is wedged

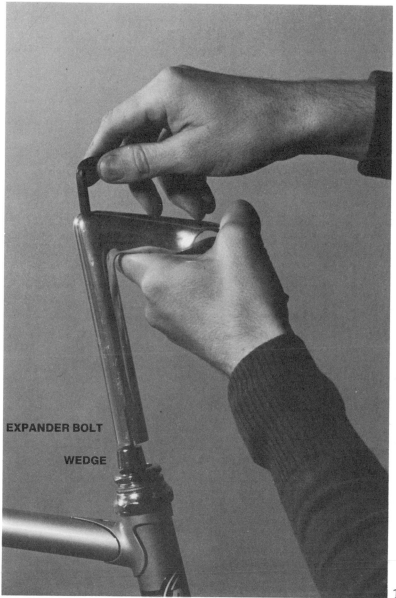

EXPANDER BOLT

WEDGE

15A

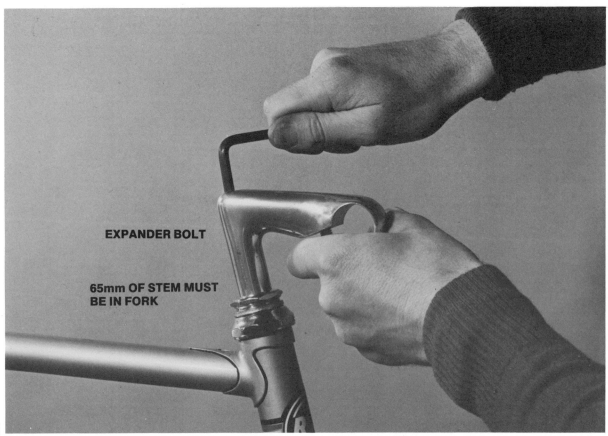

EXPANDER BOLT

65mm OF STEM MUST BE IN FORK

15B

in place, it will not come out even if the bolt is loosened. To remove a stem, unscrew the bolt a few turns. Then use a piece of cardboard to protect the finish of the bolt head and strike it with a steel hammer, straight down, using a slapping motion. This action drives down the plug, and the stem can now be twisted out of the tube.

Old stems sometimes become jammed in place by rust or dirt. Work them loose with penetrating oil. In extreme cases, if the fork crown is open at the bottom, you can drive out the plug with the end of the expander bolt, then punch up the stem with any long metal rod inserted from below. As a last resort, hammer the stem sideways while holding the fork; but remember, this does neither of them any good.

Before reinserting a clean stem of the proper size, grease it lightly. Tighten the bolt until the stem is lightly wedged, adjust it for height and direction, and then tighten it firmly but gently.

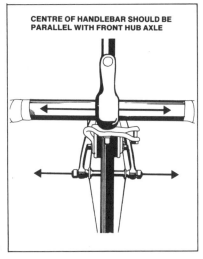

CENTRE OF HANDLEBAR SHOULD BE PARALLEL WITH FRONT HUB AXLE

16

16: Always line up handlebars with the front axle, using a section of handlebar near the stem. Lining up with the fork crown, or sighting away from the stem, may create subtle errors of alignment caused by slightly bent forks or warped bars.

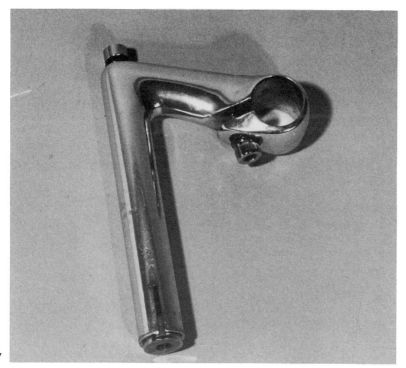

17: Most better ten-speeds have an alloy stem like this one, with an expander bolt tightened by an Allen key. Ten-speed fork columns are usually metric, but are made in slightly different sizes in different parts of the world. There is a temptation to hammer in a tight alloy stem — the metal yields easily to force — but to extract it again you will have to destroy the stem. No stem should ever have less than 65mm (2½in) of metal down in the fork tube. The minimum insertion depth is usually marked.

Handlebars

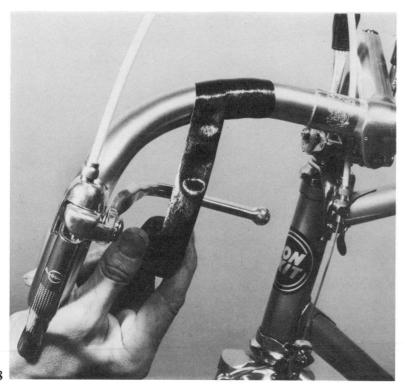

18: Non-adhesive plastic tape is the best type for general riding on a ten-speed. It is cleaner to fit, and cleaner in use. Begin high, and spiral gradually down along the bars. Clear adhesive tape can be used to anchor the top end: it will be covered by the later wrappings. Begin with a turn around the bars, then overlap each turn half the width of the tape. Wrapping in the direction shown will make for an easier grip when you are riding bare-handed on warm days.

19: At the brake lever housings, turn the tape in a figure-of-eight. Begin by spiralling down under the housing, then come up and around, and down again as shown. From here you are ready to spiral to the end of the handlebar. Tuck in the end, letting the edge protrude slightly beyond the end of the tube. Now insert the end plug, folding in the edge, and the job is done.

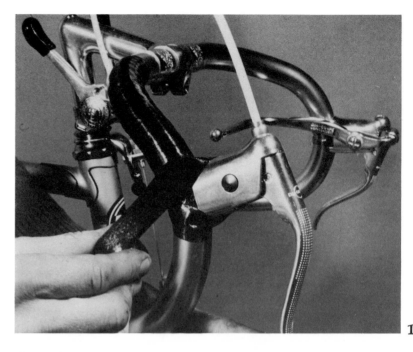

20: Conventional saddles comprise a seat pad, two stout wires, and the clamp parts shown here. Clamps are made to fit various different post sizes. Forcing a tight clamp over a large post is possible but unwise; riding with a loose clamp is uncomfortable. It will also ruin the clamp and side plate by wearing down the serrations on them.

19

Saddles

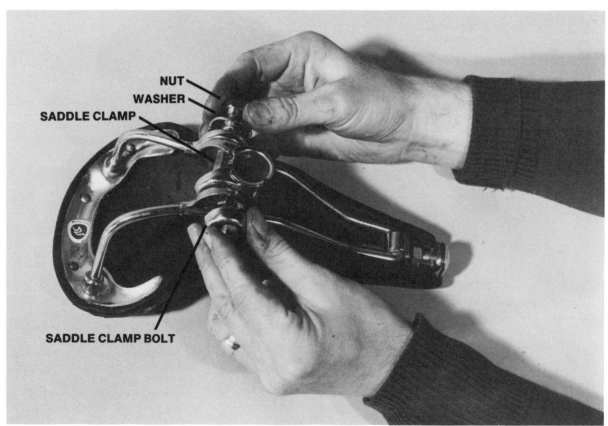

NUT

WASHER

SADDLE CLAMP

SADDLE CLAMP BOLT

20

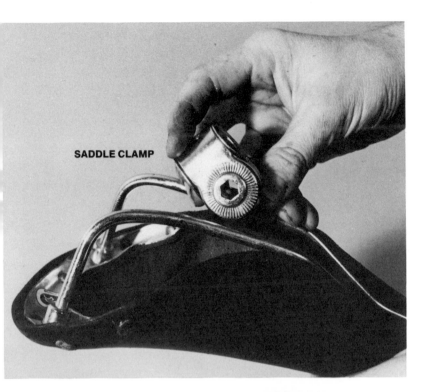

SADDLE CLAMP

21: A clamp can be turned in either direction, increasing or decreasing the distance from seat to handlebars. This is an important adjustment. On machines with upright handlebars, you will be more comfortable and have better control if you ride with your elbows slightly in front of your torso. It is also important to keep the saddle absolutely horizontal on these machines.

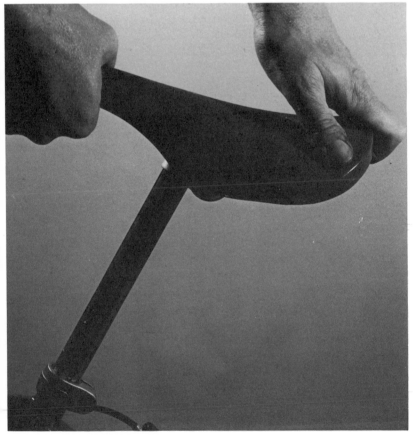

22: Seat pillars are best removed by loosening the binder bolt at the top of the seat tube, and then pulling up on the saddle (make sure it is firmly clamped). If no saddle is available, you can use vice-grip pliers, but they will almost certainly damage the finish. A pillar should be a good but not immovable fit. If it proves difficult to extract, remove the binder bolt. Insert the tip of a heavy screwdriver into the notch at the top of the tubing and prise gently to open the tubing as much as possible. That, combined with some elbow grease and some penetrating oil, should do it. Clean and lightly grease any parts you are putting back.

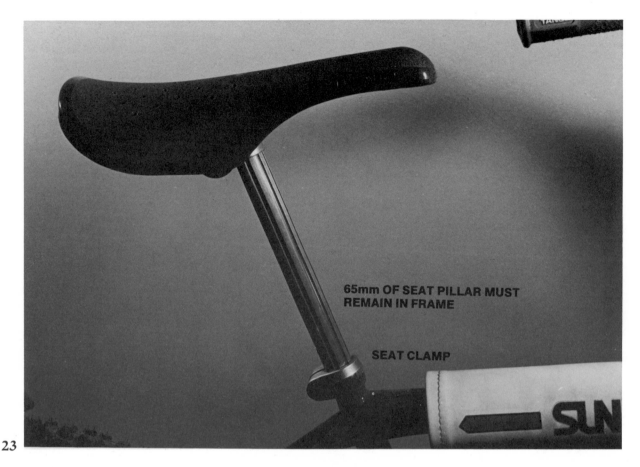

23

65mm OF SEAT PILLAR MUST REMAIN IN FRAME

SEAT CLAMP

23: A seat pillar is almost always at an angle to the forces acting on it. These can be very large. Pillars can bend or break, and have even been known to tear. A lot of pillar is exposed on machines like this BMX bike, but there is still enough inside the seat tube for safety. It is held firm by a seat clamp, common on BMX machines but rare on conventional bikes.

24: High-performance leather saddles are narrow, with tubular struts and adjustable clamps. They can also be stretched back into shape after slackening. They are best used with a special micro-adjusting seat pillar like this one. In recent years, plastic or nylon saddle tops, often lightly padded, have taken over from leather saddles.

SADDLE CLAMP

A

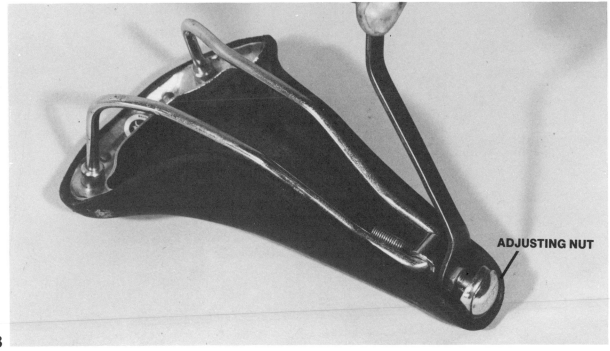

ADJUSTING NUT

B

Wheels, hubs, tyres

Hubs

If the hubs of your bicycle are in good condition, you will probably find it a satisfactory and worthwhile machine and a source of considerable pleasure. When hubs are running properly almost any other problem seems less than overwhelming. When they are not, then the machine may appear to be near the end of its useful life.

Think back to the bikes you rode in childhood. After a time the axles began to rattle, and the machine became increasingly hard to pedal; the sprockets would 'slip' when you tried to pedal forwards. It seemed like the beginning of the end. And by then you had pretty much outgrown the frame, and the machine was ready to retire to a cobwebby corner of the garage, its axle-nuts rounded by the clumsily applied spanners of junior mechanics, and its flat inner tubes decorated with commemorative patches.

But the important faults were caused by hub damage; and children are not alone in causing hub damage. If you are careless about replacing a wheel you can do just as much harm yourself. To all outward appearances, a wheel can

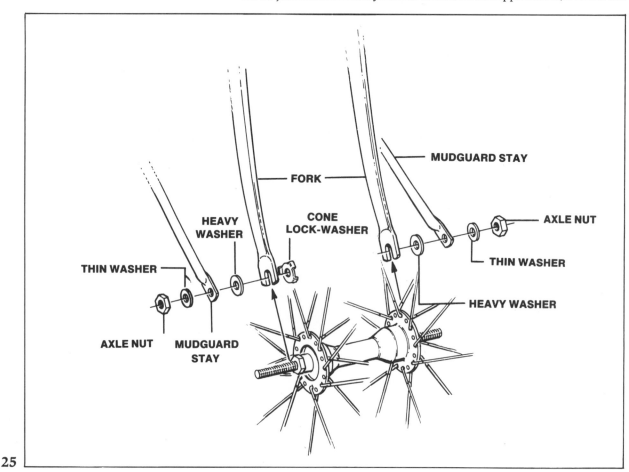

readily be fitted back into place even if a few washers are left off, or the wrong nuts used; but this can spell disaster. Fig. 25 shows a front wheel assembly from a typical child's bicycle. Notice the lock-washer that supplements the cone lock-nut inside the blade of the forks. Washers are inserted between the mudguard stays and the axle-nuts. (On an adult machine the mudguard stays might be held on an eye near each fork-end, but there might also be a mounting bracket for a cyclometer, struts for a shopping basket, or a headlight mount.)

The ears on the cone lock-washer are designed to grip the nut on one side, and to key into the fork-end. This means that the lock-washer remains motionless itself, as well as preventing movement of the lock-nut. All washers are *torque buffers*: they absorb turning force. Often they absorb differences in the vibration rate and motion of neighbouring parts — for instance, they take the squeak out of the connection of the mudguard stay next to the fork-end. In most applications they are also clutches. If a washer is positioned next to an oval or slotted mounting hole, then adjustments can be made by slightly loosening the main fastener and sliding the strut mount, for example, back and forth without disturbing the cyclometer mount. Tightening the fastener presses the washer sideways onto the strut mount, holding everything secure in the new alignment.

And that is the washer's main function. Without it, the rotation of the axle fastening nut would be transferred directly to the strut mount as the nut was tightened; the strut mount would shift out of alignment, and its metal would deform. After a few incidents like this the soft stamped metal of the strut would crack.

If the nut rotated directly at the fork-end, it would shift the axle slightly in the fork slot. If there were no washer between the fork-end and the cone lock-nut, then the bearing adjustment would change slightly. It would change rather more if the lock-nut had not been replaced and the shift of the axle were being transferred directly to the cone by friction against the fork-end. In either case, if there is no washer between the outside of the fork and the advancing axle fastening nut, there will be a slight shift of adjustment inside the fork. And even if there is a washer inside but none outside, then unless the inside washer is keyed or eared, each fastening and unfastening of the axle will affect the adjustment of the hub bearing to some extent. Since front wheels are removed more often than any other essential part of a bicycle, it follows that a good many front hubs are in poor shape.

But rear wheels are little better off. Even a multi-speed hub can open 'by itself', and cumulative errors in axle refastening account for a fair number of hub gear failures.

Checking and rebuilding hubs

Any wheel that shakes from side to side has a badly adjusted hub. Hubs are designed as precision assemblies; any sideplay that can be detected by the unaided hand or eye is bad. Grip the suspect wheel by the tyre and shake it sideways: you will feel the sideplay in your fingertips. If you can actually see it or hear it, then get ready to rebuild the hub.

If the hub is obviously dirty, take off the wheel and apply a strong detergent to the hub with a long-fibre soft brush; a car-washing brush will do.

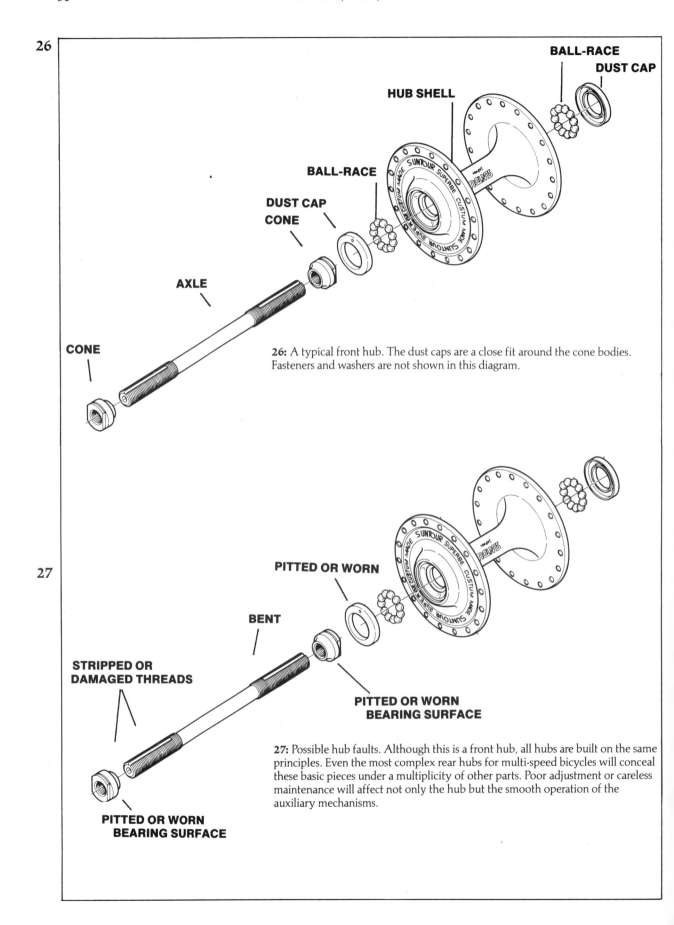

BALL-RACE

DUST CAP

HUB SHELL

BALL-RACE

DUST CAP
CONE

AXLE

CONE

26: A typical front hub. The dust caps are a close fit around the cone bodies. Fasteners and washers are not shown in this diagram.

PITTED OR WORN

BENT

STRIPPED OR
DAMAGED THREADS

PITTED OR WORN
BEARING SURFACE

27: Possible hub faults. Although this is a front hub, all hubs are built on the same principles. Even the most complex rear hubs for multi-speed bicycles will conceal these basic pieces under a multiplicity of other parts. Poor adjustment or careless maintenance will affect not only the hub but the smooth operation of the auxiliary mechanisms.

PITTED OR WORN
BEARING SURFACE

When the hub is fit to touch, take it to pieces, wiping as you go, and lay out the parts, in order, on a workbench.

Clean and dry each piece carefully, and then inspect it for wear and damage, checking against the chart (see fig. 27). Roll the axle along your bench to make sure it is straight, then check the threads. Small irregularities can be dealt with by hand-filing with the edge of a triangular file, but if sections of the thread have broken away then you will not be able to rely on future adjustments. A bent axle cannot put its bearings in proper contact with their cups, so be ruthless.

Choose a good section of axle thread, and replace the cleaned cones, lock-nuts and fasteners. Rock them with your fingertips. If they fit loosely, or turn stubbornly, on a good axle, then there is thread trouble in the part. It cannot be salvaged economically, if at all.

If the whole assembly is faulty, you may be better off buying a complete new wheel rather than attempting to rebuild it. Check the rim and spokes (page 33) to see if they need attention as well. If it seems worth rebuilding the old hub, then be sure to take all the old parts to the shop with you.

You can usually punch out the bearing cups from behind, like headset inserts. Their replacements will be a tight fit. Tap them in with a soft hammer, or lay a piece of metal across the rims, in close contact, before using a hard hammer. When the rim of the cup is level with the shell, finish seating the cup with a hardwood dowel and light hammer-taps. Special tools for inserting cups are also available.

For lubrication, follow the advice on page 14. Adjust the cones until the hub spins freely, but with no sideplay. Hold the cones with a thin cone spanner and fasten the lock-nuts. Make sure you replace the wheel properly. For routine adjustment, look at figs. 28-31.

28

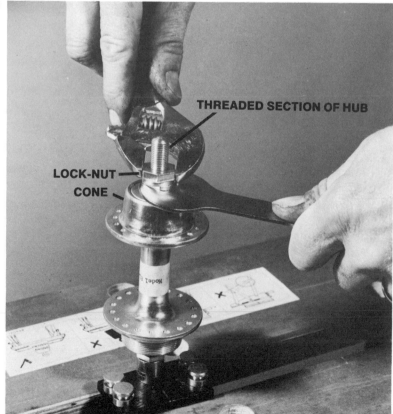

THREADED SECTION OF HUB

LOCK-NUT

CONE

28: A rear hub for a multiple freewheel. The cone is being held in place with a thin spanner so the lock-nut can be removed. If this hub were still in place in a built-up wheel, the rim of the wheel could be gripped in a vice while the hub was being dismantled horizontally. Always pad the vice with soft metal such as sheet copper. Otherwise use a special vice insert like this one, made to hold hub axles and freewheels.

29: Always remove each part separately. Any attempt to remove the cone and lock-nut together would damage the threads of every part involved.

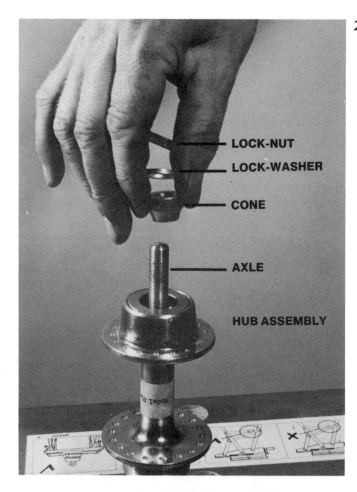

LOCK-NUT
LOCK-WASHER
CONE
AXLE
HUB ASSEMBLY

30: Dust caps are pressed lightly into hub shells. They are made of soft aluminium alloy, and should be prised out gently. Replace by tapping with a soft hammer.

31: The sprocket side of the axle in this type of hub has additional spacers, which may or may not be threaded. If they are threaded, the body may have sharp-edged grooves. The spacers compensate for the offset of the hub on the axle (see fig. 37). The threaded spacer can be changed without affecting the hub adjustment. Unthreaded spacers usually have shallow grooves.

DUST CAP
HUB SHELL

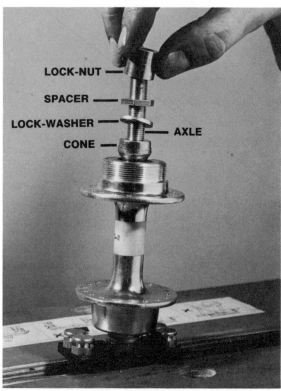

LOCK-NUT
SPACER
LOCK-WASHER
CONE
AXLE

Wheels

The rim of a wheel actually hangs from the spokes; it is part of a system in tension. Spokes can be tightened or loosened by turning their nipples — anticlockwise to tighten them, clockwise to loosen them. When the wheel is correctly tensioned, the rim is perfectly round and exactly perpendicular to the axle, the hub is at the exact centre of the wheel, and the rim does not ripple sideways when the wheel is spun.

A single loose spoke affects the entire wheel: a broken spoke affects it disastrously. Slight variations from the ideal are tolerable — and inevitable — but they lead to uneven tyre wear, poor steering, and bad caliper brake action on an otherwise sound machine. And if a wheel is out of true then the bicycle is more tiring to ride.

Most spoke problems begin when the wheel bumps over a kerb or a pothole, deforming the rim. Extreme impacts damage the rim sidewalls — normally the hub will have to be cut out of the spokes, and a new wheel built around it.

With care, rim walls can be straightened in a vice or clamp, but they are usually hollow, and tend to crumple in the process, even if the original damage is fairly slight. A wheel's best friend is good riding. Its next best friend is a spoke key of the proper size, carefully used. Spoke nipples have flats, but they are usually made of brass, and they will break if mistreated. Spokes tighten anticlockwise: do not force them, and use a smooth motion. Never try to make a major adjustment by using only a few spokes. Begin with adjustments alternately several spokes ahead of the problem and then several spokes behind it. If you are replacing spokes, follow the spoke pattern, and use identical spokes.

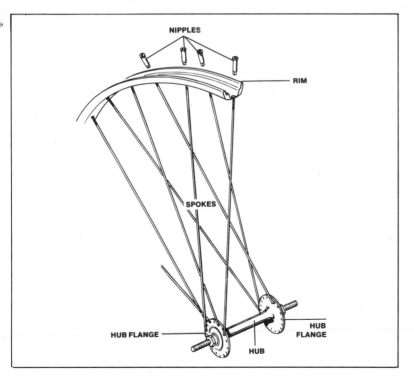

33: Be sure the spoke key (spanner) is firmly seated before attempting to turn the nipple. Keys and nipples come in many sizes; never force a fit. A nipple may be stiff because it is at the end of the threads on the spoke, or because it is frozen with dirt and spoke-rust.

34: The wheel is shown in a trueing jig. You can improvise a jig by taping a ruler across the frame stays, or by sighting against the shoes of a properly aligned caliper brake. Trueing with the tyre off gives more accurate results.

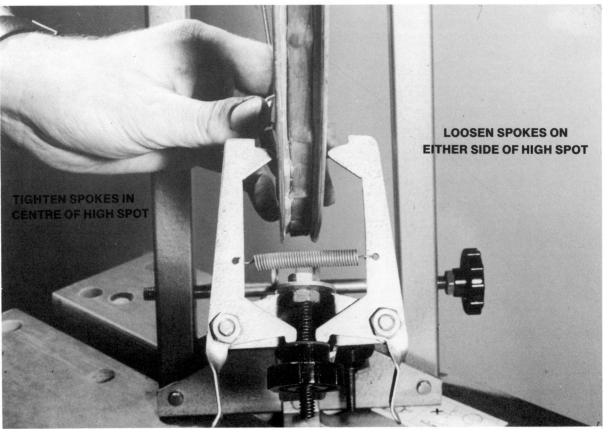

5

TO SHIFT RIM TO THE RIGHT
LOOSEN SPOKES ON THIS SIDE

TIGHTEN SPOKES ON THIS SIDE

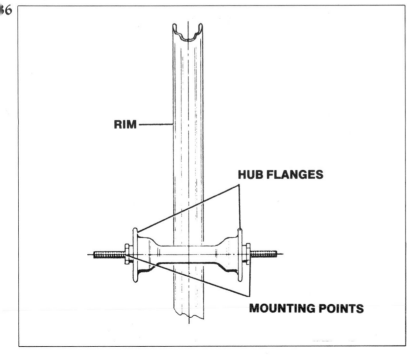

RIM

HUB FLANGES

MOUNTING POINTS

35: If a spoke nipple will not turn easily after the wheel approaches true roundness, it is frozen. Both spoke and nipple should be replaced.

36: A wheel should centre exactly between the hub lock-nuts. A small-flange wheel uses long spokes, and is more comfortable to ride. When spoking a wheel, you can bend the spoke around and under other spokes to follow the crossing pattern — it will pull straight. But do avoid twisting it.

37: The rim of a derailleur rear wheel looks off-centre. It is not, but the spokes on the right-hand side are shorter and set at a different angle from those on the left. Their ends will protrude further through the nipple unless you use shorter spokes on that side. Always trim off and file or grind spoke-ends until they are smooth and flush with the nipple crown on the inside of the rim.

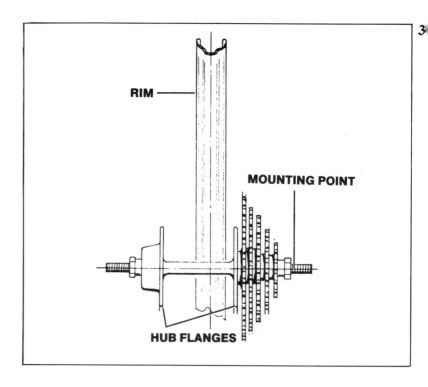

Tyre and tube repair

Flat tyres are almost always caused by cuts or punctures through the tyre and into the tube. Despite popular folklore, valves rarely fail. The second most common cause is kinking of the tube, either because it is poorly aligned with the valve hole in the rim, or because it is too big for the tyre.

Punctures are more frequent when tyres are worn. The tube can be penetrated more easily. If rim tape is not used, or if it is twisted, a rough

38: A conventional bicycle tyre with inner tube. The tyre has a U-shaped profile, and its edges are reinforced with thin wires. The tube is a separate unit with a valve moulded in. Notice the rim tape, which prevents the nipple crowns and the rough spoke-ends from rubbing through the tube.

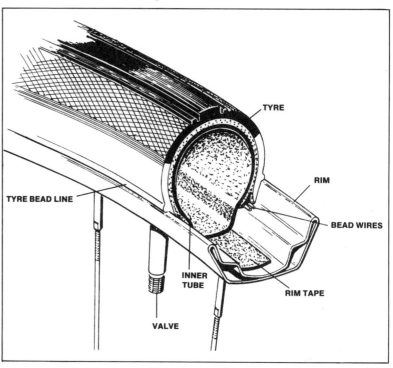

spoke-end may abrade the tube. These are the results of carelessness and bad maintenance. Rim cuts are the result of bad riding; riders who make a habit of pounding against kerbs flatten the side wall of the tyre against the edge of the rim, and the result is often a rim cut. Sometimes the surface rubber will appear to be intact even though the internal threads of the tyre are broken. The tube will push against weak spots of this kind, creating bubbles in the side wall. After a while, any of these bubbles could burst.

Keep dust out of the valve by capping it at all times.

39

START ON SIDE OPPOSITE VALVE

39: Use several tyre levers to unseat the deflated tyre. Hook them around the spokes to keep them in place.

40

WORK TYRE LEVER ALONG RIM

40: Then carefully run one lever around the bead until the tyre is unseated. Gently remove the tube.

41: Re-inflate the tube and find the leak, if necessary by immersing the tube in water. Make sure there is not more than one leak.

42: Dry and clean the tube thoroughly. Use sandpaper to roughen the area around the leak. Blow or brush away the rubber particles. Apply rubber cement, and let it dry completely.

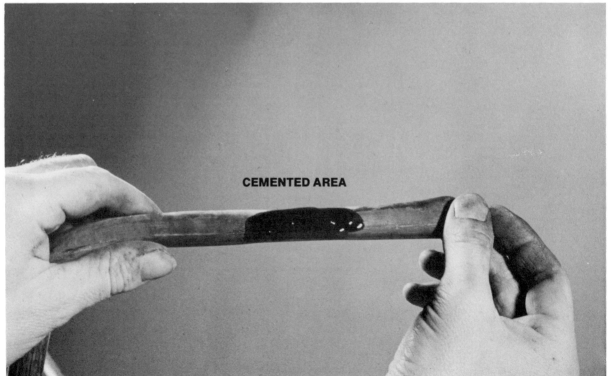

CEMENTED AREA

3

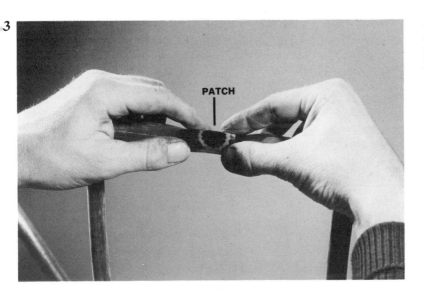

PATCH

43: Making sure your fingers are clean, carefully remove the backing from a pre-cemented patch and press on the patch meticulously.

44

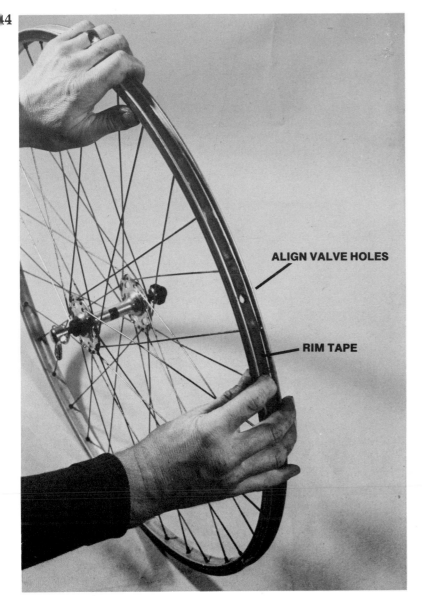

ALIGN VALVE HOLES

RIM TAPE

44: Leaving the tube to one side, align the rim tape carefully.

45: PARTIALLY INFLATE TUBE AND INSERT IN TYRE

STRETCH TYRE ONTO RIM

45: Remove all foreign objects from the tyre. Replace any tyre that has a cut which bulges under pressure. Dust the edges of the tube patch with talcum powder and insert the tube in a sound tyre of the correct size.

46: Make sure the valve stem is exactly aligned in the valve hole, and that the rim tape has not become twisted. Push the tyre on with your thumbs — never use tools. Inflate the tyre slowly, checking that the bead is properly seated.

Tubular tyres

Tubular tyres, or 'tubs', are the centre of a mystique that is all their own. Few novices own a set — you will normally only acquire them after haunting bike shops for a while, or talking to fellow enthusiasts. But if you do happen to come across a bicycle fitted with tubulars, here are a few things to bear in mind.

All tubular tyres are high-pressure tyres developed for racing or touring by advanced riders. They adhere to their unique rims by a combination of high air pressure and glue, or by double-faced adhesive tape. In the case of track racing tyres, shellac is also used.

Valves are of the Presta type; you must unscrew the knurled pin crown (see fig. 47) before the valve will operate, and you will also need an adaptor to connect the valve to a conventional air hose. Presta valves have metal bodies,

47

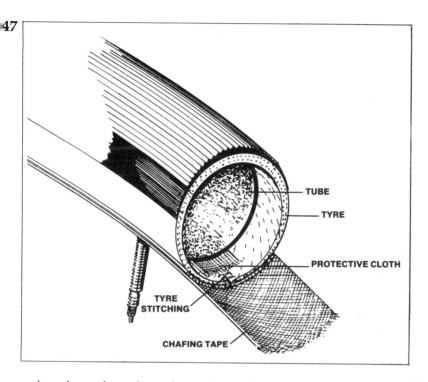

TUBE

TYRE

PROTECTIVE CLOTH

TYRE
STITCHING

CHAFING TAPE

47: The tubular or 'sew-up' tyre
developed for racing and high-speed
touring.

and are clamped into their tubes with gaskets and metal collars held down
by a nut threaded over the valve body.

The tube is thin and very pliable. The body fabric and stitching carry a
load of 100-200 psi of air pressure. The chafing tape is glued tightly over the
stitching, and acts as an extra reinforcement.

Even the best tubulars normally lose quite a bit of pressure overnight.
The tubes are often made of porous latex, and Presta valves also leak more
readily. Butyl tubes overcome this problem.

The tyre should be inspected after every use, and any embedded material

48

48: Always make the water test with the
tyre still mounted on the rim. This
minimises false leaks. Even so, some
bubbles will often emerge a long way
from the hole in the tube. Pump the tyre
hard, and watch for vigorous bubbles.

that might work through to the tube must be removed. Surface cuts of any size should be filled with tread stopping compound.

The tyre must be properly seated on the rim with a continuous light coating of good rim adhesive. A tubular tends to turn inside out when inflated, so an improperly fitted tyre will tend to roll off its rim.

A new tubular will not fit its rim until it has been stretched. A good method is to take off your shoe, hook the tyre under the arch of your foot, put your knee through the tyre, grasp the top of the tyre between your fists at the top of the thigh, and then try to straighten your leg. No need to worry about tearing the tyre in two — it won't happen.

An old tubular is unlikely to show any single fault. It will simply start to lose air faster, through accumulated micropunctures you will be unable to find. But in some cases there is clearly a single leak that justifies a repair attempt. Try to find and mark the leak on the tyre before you push the tyre off the rim with your thumbs. Work carefully and patiently. This job could well take you a full evening.

49: Once you have found the leak, remove the tyre, dry it, and work aside as little of the chafing tape as possible. Then cut the stitching carefully. Check fig. 47 — be sure your cut does not penetrate the cloth between the stitching and the tube. Now push the cloth aside and reach gently for the tube.

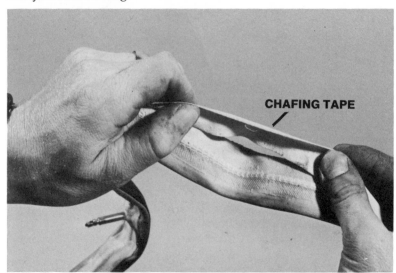

CHAFING TAPE

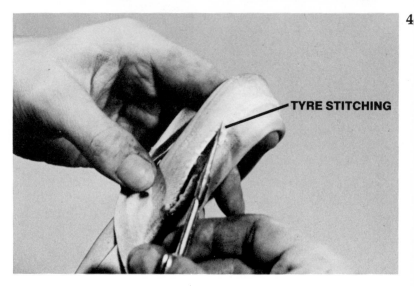

TYRE STITCHING

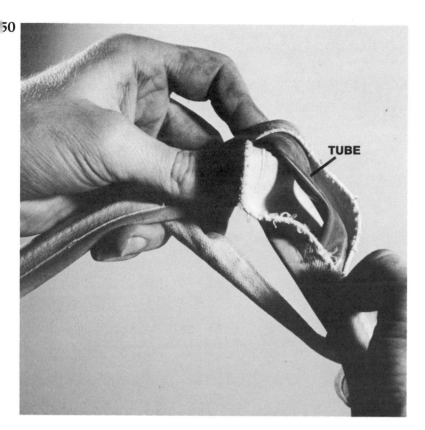

50: If handled roughly, the tube will tear as you try to work a loop out through the cut in the stitching.

51: Patching is done in the same way as for an ordinary tube, but the patches are thinner and smaller.

52

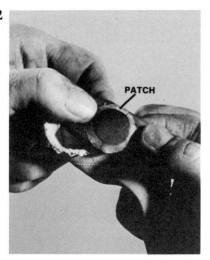

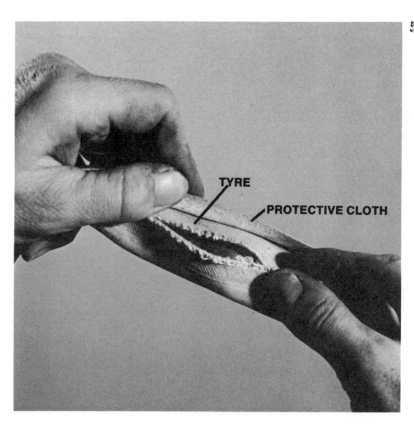

52: Place the patch precisely, then dust it with talc to prevent the tube sticking to the tyre.

53: Carefully reinsert the loop of tube, pulling at the tyre to help it settle in. Then replace the cloth. On some tyres, the cloth is lightly stitched in, and you will have had to cut these stitches, too. Replace them with tacking stitches of ordinary sewing thread.

54: Using a repair kit, or a sailmaker's needle and thread, sew back carefully through the old holes. Draw the edges of the tyre firmly back together — do not leave gaps or buckles. Avoid rolling up the chafing tape, as this must now be glued back flat over the stitching. Be meticulous about this. Test the tyre by partially inflating it and leaving it overnight. If it is sound, remount it carefully.

Chainwheels, cranks and chains

Three-piece cranksets

The classic steel three-piece crankset is held together by the cotter pins. To remove a cotter, unscrew the fastening nut until it is level with the end of the pin. Hit the nut sharply straight down with a hard hammer. Then remove the nut and washer. Tap gently to finish taking out the pin, using a blunt punch if necessary.

To reassemble, nudge the cotter pin back into place with easy taps of a soft hammer, and draw it in fully by tightening the nut. Be sure the pin faces the flats on the spindle.

In this assembly, the bearing cones are the flanges at each end of the axle. Check their cup-side bases for excessive wear. When replacing an axle, remember that many axles of the same diameter can be purchased with different lengths on the chainwheel side.

Most cups are conventionally ('right-hand') threaded, but most English left cups are left-hand threaded. This is an attempt to overcome the tendency of these sets to unwind their cups if the bearing jams with dirt, or its lubricant dries out.

The right or 'fixed' cup is often tacked in with a drop of molten brass. Clean out the right cup with a rag on a dowel and a fingertip through the axle hole if the cup does not need replacement. Use a safe solvent, and be sure to clean out the left cup threads in the bracket as well.

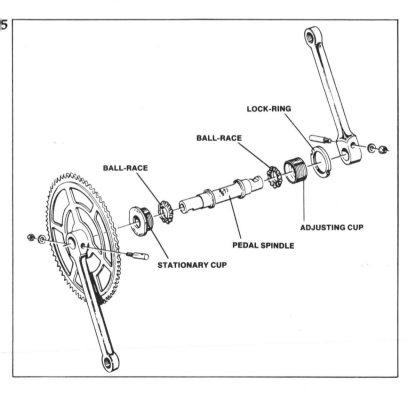

LOCK-RING

BALL-RACE

BALL-RACE

ADJUSTING CUP

PEDAL SPINDLE

STATIONARY CUP

55: The classic three-piece crankset, so called because the axle, the left crank and the chainwheel crank are separate components. Notice the cotter pins, which have flat faces that press against the flats on the axle. Notice also that the chainwheel side of the axle extends further beyond the cone flange than the left crank side does. (The chainwheel is considered to be on the right-hand side of the bicycle — i.e. looking from the back.)

56: This lock-ring spanner is shown in use after the crank has been removed. The left-hand adjusting cup and its lock-ring both have a right-hand thread. The right-hand cup, which is fixed, has a left-hand thread on British frames. If a lock-ring spanner is not available, the lock-ring can be moved by inserting a punch sideways in one of the key slots and tapping it with a hammer, but this often damages the slot. This particular cup is keyed; others may also carry flats for a wrench. Compare the lock-ring spanner with the multispanner in fig. 3.

57: Once the lock-ring is removed, the cup can be screwed out. Just in case loose balls have been used, always tilt an unfamiliar bottom bracket so that the balls cannot fall into the tubes, and keep the axle pressed back in the assembly so that the balls of the fixed cup will stay in place until you are ready to deal with them. Cups and axles like these are in common use on all types of frame.

58: When removing the axle, you may be lucky enough to find that the ball-race comes out as well. Be prepared for other things, though. If the balls are loose, check that none are embedded in old grease at the bottom of the right-hand cup. If the frame tubes are open to the bottom bracket it is worth plugging them with wads of soft paper after cleaning out the bracket. Then fit a plastic liner into the curve of the bracket tube before reassembling. These precautions will stop dirt entering the assembly in future, and promote a better distribution of the lubricant.

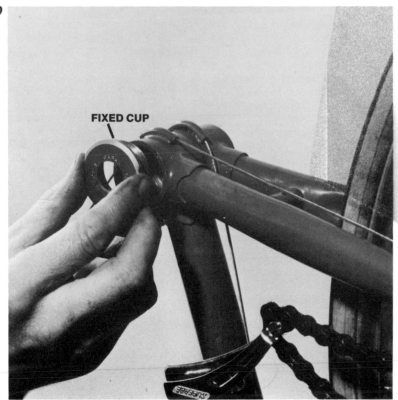

59: The fixed cup will be harder to remove, even if it has not been brazed in place. One method is to clamp it in a vice and push on the frame. Be sure of the thread direction before applying full force, and do not remove it at all unless it is absolutely necessary.

One-piece cranksets

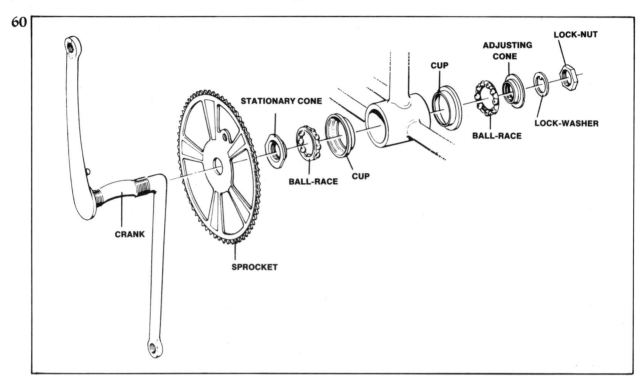

60: The one-piece crankset is easily identified by the streamlined look of the cranks and the large diameter of the bottom bracket tubing. If the parts on the left side — the lock-nut, the lock-washer, the adjusting cone, etc. — are removed, the Z-shaped crank can be twisted and removed through the bottom bracket. The remaining parts can then be removed. Unlike most three-piece cranksets, this one can be slipped on and off its key. Replacement chainwheels in larger sizes can be used to step up the gearing on a child's bike that would otherwise be outgrown. Notice that the bearing set is very similar to a head set laid on its side. It can be worked on and adjusted in much the same way, except that either the lock-nut or the adjusting cone will be left-hand threaded. The one-piece crankset is used for the majority of BMX bikes.

61: The first step in removing a one-piece crank. Be careful about removing this lock-nut — its washer is easily damaged.

62: One-piece sets always use caged bearings and pressed-in cups. The cup often shows a wide streak of polished metal that stands out from the matt finish of its material. This is not a sign of excessive wear unless the bearings have ground an irregular groove.

63

63: There is always some angle that will allow the crank to be pulled through the bracket. Punching out the left cup ahead of time can sometimes help in difficult cases.

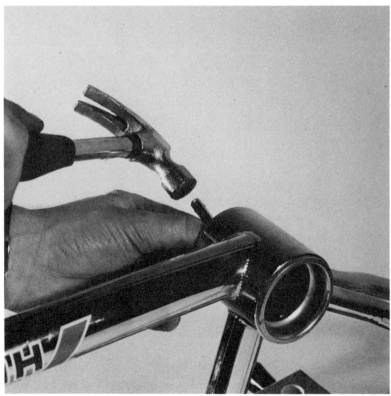

64: If necessary you can easily punch out the cups. On some children's cycles the cups lie behind riveted dust caps, and no work can be done until the rivets have been drilled out. Afterwards the holes can be tapped for machine screws, so that the dust caps can be replaced. If the metal of the bottom bracket is soft enough, self-tapping screws can be used. Make sure the screw-ends do not protrude against the cups — they might move or deform them.

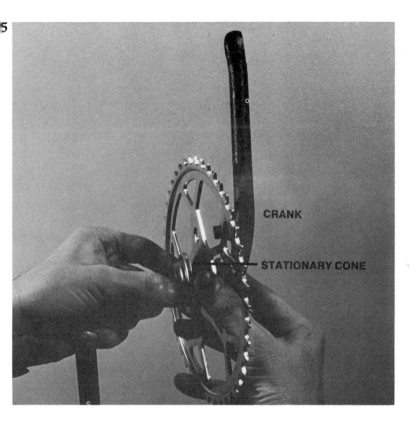

65: Removing the stationary cone this way could hardly be easier. The chainwheel will now slip off.

Cotterless cranksets

Cotterless cranksets are a racing design, but they are now used on almost all sports and touring bicycles. The cranks are held in exact opposition, and once they have been fully drawn onto their axle ends by tightening the mounting bolts, they will often stay in place by friction, even if the bolts work loose.

To remove a cotterless unit you will need a special tool, which consists of a threaded bolt inside a threaded body (see fig. 3). When the cap and the mounting bolt have been removed, the threaded body screws into the dust cap threads. After this body is seated, the central bolt is screwed in. It pushes against the axle end, and the arm is pushed off (see figs. 67-70).

Alloy cranksets have several special characteristics that are an advantage in high-performance cycling. They are lighter than steel sets, more sizes of chainwheel are made to fit their spiders (their crank arms), and an alloy set is less susceptible to the subtle ripples that steel sets often develop after a period of use.

However, alloy is softer then the steel of the pedal axles and the crank-extractors that thread into it. It strips readily. It also 'freezes' or binds to itself and to other metals. The dust caps, if installed dry, will often strip out their threads instead of loosening, and will have to be chiselled out. Most keen cyclists ride without dust caps, which means the threads must be carefully cleaned before the cranks are extracted.

To avoid most of these problems it is worth lightly greasing all threads. Be sure not to dull any threads by using thick-wall spanners on the bolt heads.

66

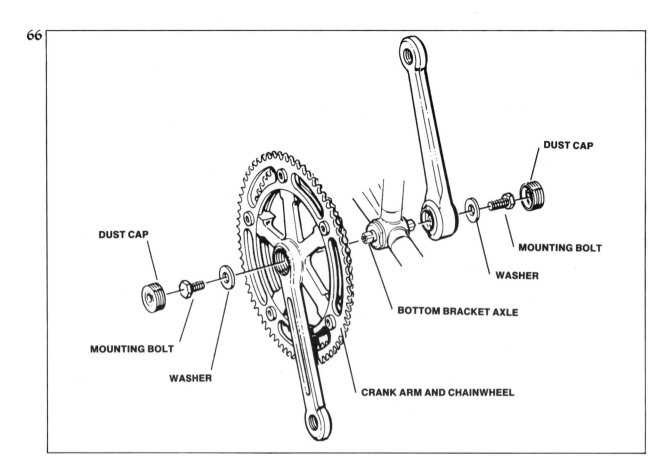

DUST CAP

DUST CAP

MOUNTING BOLT

WASHER

MOUNTING BOLT

WASHER

BOTTOM BRACKET AXLE

CRANK ARM AND CHAINWHEEL

67

DUST CAP

WASHER

AXLE-END BOLT

66: The external parts of cotterless cranksets are nearly always made of aluminium alloy. The bearing set is a normal three-piece design. The axle ends are chamfered into keys to fit the crank arms, which are held on by bolts concealed under dust caps.

67: The first stage in removing a cotterless crank: taking off the dust cap using an Allen key or an L-spanner. This is a Japanese SunTour Superbe set with a five-armed spider and two chainwheels. Use the extractor tool appropriate to your own crankset. Notice how all the chainwheel components bolt into place: the Superbe and the Campagnolo use shoulder nuts sunk through the rings and spider arms. A small screwdriver can be used to hold them while you fasten the bolts from the other side. Another popular design is the six-armed TA set. On cheaper cotterless sets you may find an external alloy chainguard ring.

68: The axle-end bolt and washer have been removed with a special spanner (see figs. 3 and 70): it is designed not to rub against the threads for the dust cap. If these threads become dull they may have to be re-tapped at a shop to avoid future problems. A sure-handed mechanic can try to re-establish the alloy threads by carefully inserting the extractor, but an alignment error could actually make things worse.

69: The extractor body can now be screwed into the cap threads with the central bolt, or extractor screw, wound back. The main reason for removing a crank is to maintain the bottom bracket set. On Superbe and Campagnolo sets chainrings can be removed without disturbing the cranks. This is not possible with TA sets.

70: The extractor screw is now wound in, and pushes at the axle-end. If the extractor body is not all the way in on the cap threads, or has been cross-threaded, the force of the turning screw will now tear out the extractor body. If the cap threads are ripped out, the crank arm has to be prised off the axle — normally it will be ruined. Despite these dreadful possibilities, cotterless cranksets are very popular on high-performance machines, and thousands of people repair or maintain them successfully every day.

Repairing bent components

Chainwheels, cranks and cotters are often the victims of a great deal of banging and bending. Obvious deformities can be dealt with at once, but some are subtle enough to pass unnoticed, and in the long run these will affect performance.

A chainwheel has two functions. One is to pull the chain around, the other is to maintain an appropriate chain line (see figs. 87-89 and the chapter on derailleurs (pages 65-69) for more detail). A bent chainwheel will ripple the chain line; at best this creates energy losses and excess wear, at worst it can throw off the chain.

Check the precision of the system by turning the cranks by hand. Watch for bent or loose cranks and pedals, bent spiders, and especially bent chainwheels.

Bent chainwheels can often be repaired by laying them flat on a block of soft wood, a thick, stone-free lawn, or wet sand, and then tapping them flat with a hammer. The last few ripples will be maddeningly persistent, but even these can be removed given time and patience.

Individual bent teeth can be straightened with pliers. Any rough spots should be carefully filed by hand. Worn teeth develop a hooked profile, and will refuse to accept new chain. It is possible to regrind all the teeth, but this is hardly a practical solution. It is better to replace the chainwheel.

Bent cranks can be trued in a shop, and pedals with oversized spindles are made for cranks that have been stripped and re-tapped. Unfortunately they are not easy to find.

Replacement cotter pins must be exactly the right size. The flat wedging face will almost certainly need to be filed a little for the final, perfect fit.

71: Chainwheels are often designed to be replaceable, either for repair or so that tooth-counts can be altered to give a more satisfactory gear ratio. Shown here is a steel set with a fixed (permanently mounted) spider. Three-speed and five-speed chainwheel/spider units are normally fixed to the crank, and cannot be taken apart. All but the least expensive ten-speed machines have removable chainwheels. Fifteen- and eighteen-speed machines use three chainwheels, but apart from that are built up in the same way as ten-speed assemblies.

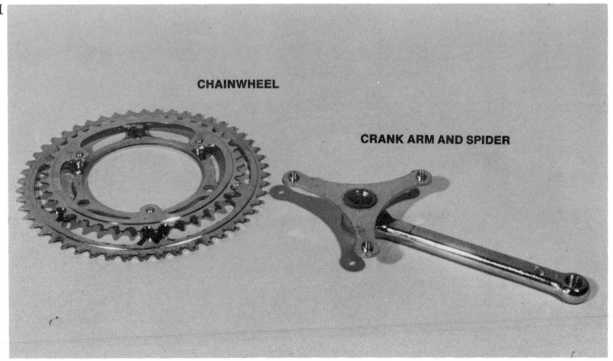

71

CHAINWHEEL

CRANK ARM AND SPIDER

72

72: Instead of shoulder nuts, steel chainwheels often use positioning flanges and bolting threads cut into the metal of the spider.

73: The struts of the new chainwheel drop onto the flanges, and the mounting screws bolt through into the spider arms.

73

MOUNTING SCREW

Pedals

Most pedals are sealed throwaway units of fair to middling quality as systems. Few pedals last long enough in service for their bearing problems to reveal themselves: impacts of one sort or another, bent spindles, or stripped spindle-end threads, will normally take their toll first.

Little can be done to service most pedals. An occasional drop of light oil has to suffice. Other repairs are limited to tightening or replacing the through-bolt assemblies that hold the rubber blocks in place on rubber pedals.

'Rat-trap' or blockless pedals appear on many ten-speeds, with or without the toe-clips that many cyclists seem to find essential. On the more expensive 'tourer' ten-speeds, there will be a removable dust cap giving access to a spindle set that can be serviced just like any other bearing assembly.

At the other end of the quality spectrum is the bolt-through pedal normally fitted to toddlers' bikes. Here the spindle end is a bolt through the crank arm, held by a nut and washer at the inward face of the crank. Systems of this type tend to unwind themselves. Sometimes they are also seen on replacement pedals, where the original pedal has stripped the spindle mounting hole in the crank. A more usual cure, normally done by a shop, is to tap out the crank in a larger size (see page 55).

A very sticky or wobbly pedal can be a serious impediment to good riding, not to mention the likelihood of its causing knee injury. Pedal service and/or replacement is important, and can be a way to improve the performance of a recalcitrant machine dramatically. It is easy to substitute high-performance pedals for standard types, except that here, as with other components, Italian and French metric types appear to be interchangeable but will only produce jam fits (see page 91). As noted on page 55, one-piece cranks use a narrow-spindle pedal. Apart from these relatively minor discrepancies, pedals from one manufacturer will freely substitute for those from another. All left pedals have left-hand threads, and all right pedals have

74: High-performance pedals use the stationary cone/adjustable cone principle which we have already seen in the bottom bracket. The cone must be adjusted and then held in place with needle-nose pliers. Push the washer down firmly, then tighten the lock-nut smoothly with a small spanner or with pliers. A thin-walled socket on a jointed extension is often used. The two body bolts are fasteners for a toe-clip (not shown).

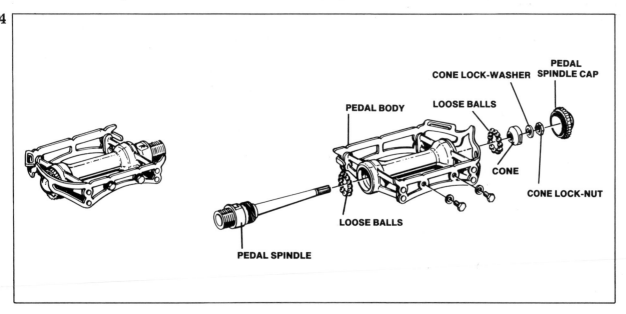

PEDAL SPINDLE CAP
CONE LOCK-WASHER
PEDAL BODY
LOOSE BALLS
CONE
CONE LOCK-NUT
LOOSE BALLS
PEDAL SPINDLE

right-hand threads. For alloy cranks use pedals with a longer thread than that used for steel cranks.

Always fit pedals carefully. If a pedal cannot be threaded on by hand for quite a few turns, it is probably the wrong size. However, there may be dirt in the threads, or the threads may be damaged.

Always grease the threads lightly. Minor thread damage in steel cranks can sometimes be dealt with by inserting the pedal from the other side, then unscrewing it again.

Master-linked chain

7

MASTER LINK

75: Chains for many bicycles with only one rear sprocket have a master or connecting link with a removable side plate. All chains have side plates connected by rivets passing through the rollers. In the master link, the rivets are replaced by two studs permanently fixed to the inside plate and passing through the open rollers of the two adjacent links. There are grooves near the ends of the studs. Some master side plates simply snap into these grooves, and can be removed by bending the link between your thumbs to make the studs turn inwards a little. The type shown here uses an elongated C clip to retain the plate after it has been fitted over the ends of the studs. The clip can be pushed off sideways. The two types are not interchangeable.

77: A chain works most effectively when it runs in a line parallel to the long axis of the bicycle. On derailleur machines, of course, this is impossible, but on all other bicycles an ideal line can be achieved by replacing the bottom bracket axle with one of a better length, or by re-spacing the sprockets. Most rear sprockets are dished, and can be turned over to move the chain line in or out.

6

AXLE NUT

76: When replacing the wheel, make sure it is positioned exactly between the chainstays. Adjust and hold it steady with the axle-nuts slightly slack, then tighten them.

7

78

78: A slack chain will not run properly. Nor will an excessively tight chain. Chains of this type should almost invariably have 10 mm (⅜ in) of play, as shown here. Move the rear axle in the fork-end slots until the play is correct.

Derailleur chain

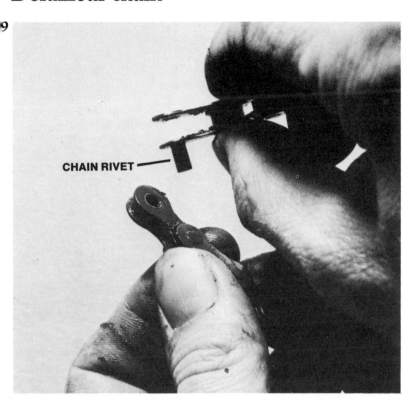

CHAIN RIVET

79: Bicycle chain looks deceptively simple. Each link is made up of two side plates, two rivets, two rivet bushes inside the rollers, and two rollers. Derailleur chain is particularly ingenious because it has to be thin and strong, yet supple enough to whip up and down the sprockets (see figs. 104 ff).

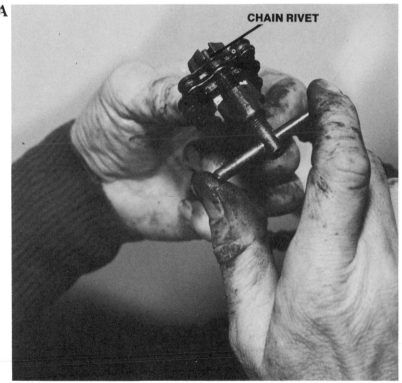

CHAIN RIVET

80: Derailleur chain has no master link. It can be 'cut' (opened) at any link by pushing out a rivet until it is clear of everything but one side plate. The chain can be relinked by turning the chain over in the tool and pushing the rivet through until it is jam-fitted back into the opposite side plate.

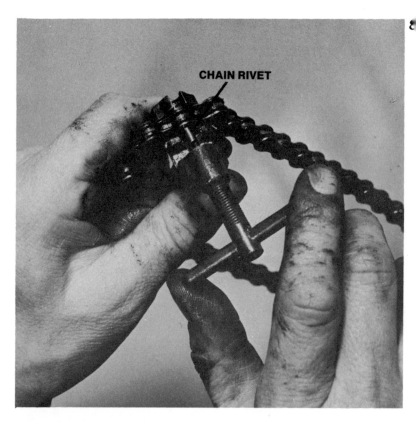

2

82: Chain that has been twisted in an accident can be straightened between two spanners. Work carefully to restore the straightness of the side plates. Test by fitting the chain and cranking the sprockets slowly by hand, feeling for rough action link by link.

81: The chain-riveting tool shown in fig. 80 has two positions for the chain, one for pushing the rivet in and out, and another for loosening the link. It is not a heavy-duty tool — follow the instructions supplied with it. Practise on scrap chain from the rubbish bin at your cycle shop.

These methods can be used to add or remove links on any chain. Old chain is always stretched — new links cannot be inserted successfully. The teeth on old sprockets are worn into their chain; if the old chain has been used for a long time, replacing it may also mean replacing the sprockets.

Never lubricate chain heavily. Heavy grease traps abrasive dirt. On master-linked chain, use a little light oil or petrol. Petrol or dry molybdenum spray are good for derailleur chain. Silicone-based lubricants break down and become abrasive with age.

83

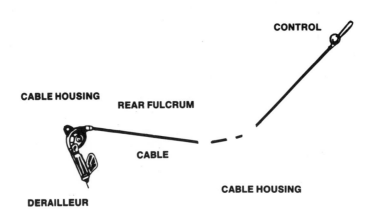

CONTROL

CABLE HOUSING   REAR FULCRUM

CABLE

CABLE HOUSING

DERAILLEUR

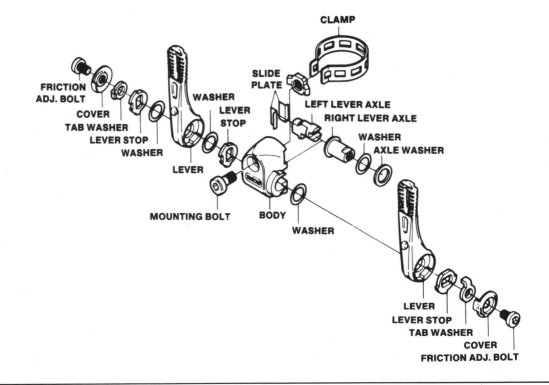

CLAMP

SLIDE
PLATE

FRICTION
ADJ. BOLT   WASHER

LEVER
COVER   STOP
TAB WASHER
LEVER STOP
WASHER

LEVER

LEFT LEVER AXLE
RIGHT LEVER AXLE

WASHER
AXLE WASHER

MOUNTING BOLT   BODY

WASHER

LEVER
LEVER STOP
TAB WASHER
COVER
FRICTION ADJ. BOLT

Derailleur controls

Cable controls combine lightness, strength and flexibility. Over the years, other systems for operating caliper brakes and gear-changing mechanisms have gradually fallen into disuse. Cable systems reign supreme — despite a considerable number of disadvantages.

Cable controls rely on tension. Every anchor point in the system is constantly being pulled, or pushed to balance a pull somewhere else. Slack anywhere in the system can cripple it completely. If the system is to work properly then every anchor, clamp and spring must be operating perfectly.

Cable stretches by its very nature. Because it is wound from spiral strands it has unmatched durability and a strength no solid wire could approach; but for the same reason any tension at the ends will tend to pull the strands into line, lengthening the cable. As a result, no cable adjustment is permanent.

Cable ends soon fray, and become very difficult to pass through clamps and anchors. Cables on new bicycles are capped with plastic or lead, but these caps are soon lost, and must in any case be removed while pulling the cable out of the sheath to lubricate it.

Cable rusts, and so do the spiral-wound flat steel coils inside cable sheathing. Unfortunately only steels prone to rust are suitable for this use.

These problems can be overcome. Cables can be lubricated by dabbing your palm with white grease and running the cable through it. This will protect the sheath, too. Cable-ends can be soldered. The anchor points in the system can be checked regularly. New cable stretches dramatically, but after a while it settles down to the point where any further stretch can be accommodated by resetting the adjusters built into all cable systems.

Cable systems have sheaths at many points along the system. These guide the cable in wide curves that reduce the friction of the cable against its guides. The single piece of sheathing between a brake-lever housing and the first anchor on the top tube does the work of at least three pulleys — and does it better.

By screwing out the adjusters at the ends of some sheaths you can effectively lengthen the sheaths. This makes the cable travel further around the curve of the sheathing, and so takes slack out of the system. The adjusting barrels on rear hub gear control cables do the same thing; they wind the barrel farther on or off the adjusting screw attached to the pull chain or bell crank. They also allow you to remove the wheel without taking apart the entire system or (in theory at least) disturbing the adjustments.

Derailleur cables, anchors and sheaths tend to be more delicate than those used in brake systems, but otherwise there are no important differences. In both systems the cables are often bared, when it is possible to do so, by stopping the sheaths at the beginning of straight runs. This avoids friction and lessens (microscopically!) the overall weight of the bicycle. This can be more important than it sounds to racing enthusiasts, who weigh parts to the nearest milligram.

Bared cable may snag, and if it does it tends to operate its control — change a gear or apply a brake. But this is a rare occurrence; besides, bare cables tend to make a multi-speed bicycle with caliper brakes look that much less like a vine-trellis.

83 (opposite): Typical ten-speed rear derailleur controls are seen here on the bicycle and in exploded view. At lower right is the control for the front derailleur, which is mounted on the seat tube. The two systems are basically mirror images of one another. The control mount shown here is clamped around the down tube; another common form of mounting is brazing directly to the tube. Other mounts occur on the handlebar stem or at the handlebars themselves instead of end plugs. Commonest is the continuous tension control: it is never lubricated, and depends on pressure at the tension cup. The click-stop type, with internal ratchets and springs, is also popular. The continuous control is very much like a tuning peg on a guitar or a violin — it will place the chain anywhere between the lowest and the highest derailleur positions. Click-stop types operate very much like hub-gear controls.

If brakes operate stiffly and stay closed, or if controls will not stay in adjustment, check the cables first. What may seem like a brake spring problem or something dire inside the hub might be no more than cable friction or a loose anchor.

If a ten-speed changes gear for no apparent reason, start by checking the control tension adjustment. You may have a loose anchor at the gear lever, but the chances are that you need to tighten the tension thumbscrew very slightly. (If you don't have a thumbscrew, adjust the slotted bolt head.) The other possibility is that someone has lubricated the gear lever for you. In that case, the only thing to do is to take it apart and wash it thoroughly in solvent.

A common cause of jamming is a broken strand inside a sheath. If this happens to you on the road, pull out the cable and unwind both ends of the strand along the total length of the cable. Break off the top end at the base of the anchor-ball moulded to that end. Then rethread the cable. But remember that it needs replacing as soon as possible; and try to find out why that strand broke in the first place. The sheath may have a broken coil, in which case you will need to replace the sheath as well. Any kink in a sheath is an early sign of trouble to come, and any break in the elastic outer skin will soon become a pit of rust.

Trim replacement cables and sheaths to length with sharp, well-made cut-

84: Stem-fitting levers are easily accessible: the levers are longer than usual, so that they reach slightly above handlebar height. Otherwise the assembly is much the same as the one shown in fig. 95.

85: Controls in the conventional location on the down tube. On some sets, the thumbscrew adjusting ring is slotted for a screwdriver blade. The tension should be firm but not hard.

86: At the other end of the cable is the short rear sheath that houses the cable between the rear stop, or fulcrum, and the derailleur. This occasionally clogs up with dirt and must be cleaned out. A few bicycles avoid this by sheathing the cable all the way from the levers to the derailleur, but this does introduce more friction.

87: If you are replacing or re-tensioning any part of a derailleur system, make sure all the adjusters are wound in before you start. When anchoring the cable-end (as here) leave enough extra cable to grasp for future tightening. Coil the excess length and solder or cap the end.

CABLE ANCHOR BOLT

GUIDE

88: Some front derailleurs bring the sheath up to a stop and anchor the cable above it. The sheath must be cut to an exact length. Too short, and the cable will bind at the curve; too long, and the bottom bracket shell will distort the curve. For this reason most modern sports bikes use an unsheathed cable like the one shown here, which passes underneath a guide before rising to the clamping point.

ting pliers, using a decisive action. Leave the ends clean. If you know how to use a soldering iron, fill the end with solder for about a quarter of an inch, then sand it smoothly back to its original diameter.

In cutting the sheath, you may not have been able to avoid bending the end in. Ream out the sheath-end with an awl, or the end of a tapered punch, and then file the edge to a neat finish.

The metal collars at the ends of cables are called ferrules. Cable sheathing and cable come in a variety of diameters; so do ferrules. Some ferrules are parts of adjusters. Others are made to fit into the ferrule-like ends of adjusters. Some ferrules, for instance those made to fit into the selector ends of Sturmey-Archer sheathing, and those for brake sheaths that terminate in non-adjusting stops, will have nipples made to enter sockets of various types. A sheath-end without a ferrule will appear to work, but in fact it will be crushing its end and pinching the cable.

Always be sure that the cable diameter matches the inside diameter of the sheath. Make sure the ferrules match it, too.

Oversized cable will bind in the sheath; undersized cable will wear through the coils and then fray on the breaks.

CABLE ANCHOR BOLT

CABLE

89: Provided that all anchors, stops and guides are tight, the major problem with derailleur controls is dirt in the sheaths (if used) and in the operating linkages of the derailleurs. Because of their location, the major components of the system are vulnerable to silt; on wet rides it will seep into every crack, drying into a hard cement. You can hear it grind! Thorough washing is the only cure.

Cable-operated brakes

Brake controls

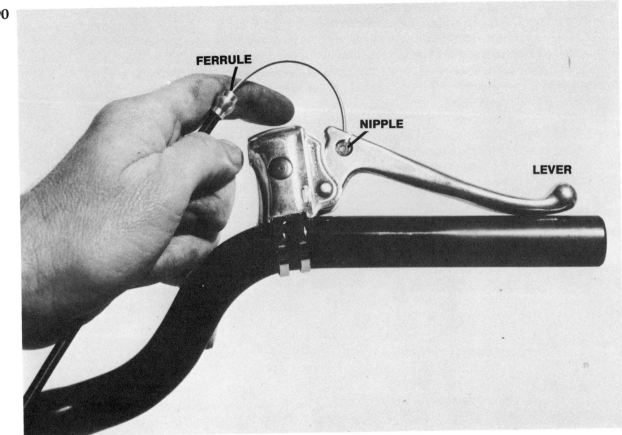

90

90: Often you will not need to unsheathe a cable in order to remove it. This touring brake-lever assembly is slotted at the ferrule entry and at the nipple anchorage. Just take the tension off the cable and slip it free at the controls. Pinching the brake stirrups together often gives you enough slack.

92: Drop-handlebar levers, whether or not they have the upper linkage, fasten to the bar with a wraparound clamp tightened by the tensioner screw behind the brake cable. The receiver for the cable end nipple is slotted. Since it pivots, you may need to hold it in place with the tip of a screwdriver while the nipple is being inserted.

1

NYLON BUSHING

DUAL LEVER

NYLON BUSHING

SCREW

2

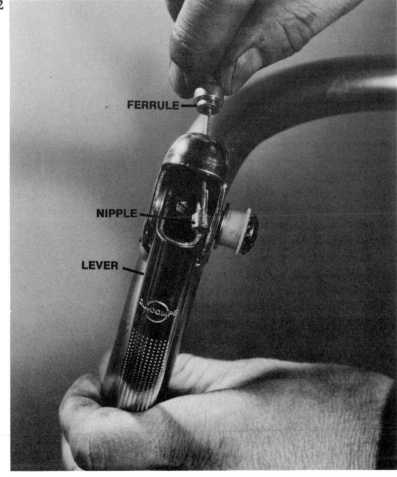

FERRULE

NIPPLE

LEVER

91: The increasingly popular dual lever control linkage, or 'safety lever', for drop-handlebar bicycles. Check it regularly for wear and for loosening of the various parts of the upper lever: this linkage needs to be precise to be of any use at all. Notice the nylon bushing. Plastic or metal bushings are often used in bicycle assemblies to lessen, or even avoid, the need for lubrication. Nylon is excellent for this purpose.

ADJUSTING BARREL

QUICK-RELEASE CAM

93: A cam-type quick-release for centre-pull brakes. A flip of the thumb lever moves the ferrule up or down. This assembly also features an adjusting barrel. Not all assemblies have this feature, but all the components are designed to fit together, so existing systems can always be upgraded. This one is shown fitted in the place of the front hanger stud (see fig. 1). The lower quick-release cam operates on the straddle bridge.

95: Some cable carriers or 'straddle bridges' are open, like this one, and can also be used for quick-release. The anchorages for the straddle cable are often slotted for quick-release — here they are slotted on the inner face. Straddle cables on other models end in one ball and one clamp, so that the straddle cable can be quick-released and re-tensioned easily. Many high-performance side-pull brakes for use with drop-handlebar machines have a quick-release built into the caliper.

REAR CABLE HANGER

94: Quick-release can also be achieved simply by pulling any convenient sheath-end out of a slotted stop. This is why few side-pull brakes with tourist levers have quick-release fittings — it is easier to release at the lever.

Notice the rear cable hanger and adjuster. Quick-release is also possible here by using the Weinmann cam-operated type shown, fitted to the seat clamp bolt.

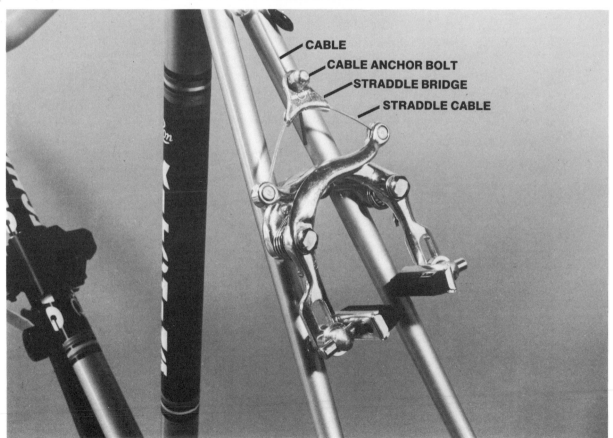

CABLE
CABLE ANCHOR BOLT
STRADDLE BRIDGE
STRADDLE CABLE

Centre-pull brakes

The centre-pull brake is self-adjusting, reliable, and has excellent stopping power. In racing circles, where every fraction of a gram of weight is considered, high-performance side-pulls have been growing popular, but there is no better means of stopping a bicycle than two well-maintained centre-pull brakes. And centre-pulls, like side-pulls, are easy to repair, and readily accessible for inspection and service.

However, fig. 96 reveals the catalogue of horrors that can afflict the centre-pull brake, or any complex system subject to occasional sudden acute stresses. There are a number of points at which sudden or subtle damage can occur, but parts for repair are readily available from almost any bicycle shop, and are inexpensive and easily assembled. Just make absolutely certain that the replacement part is precisely the right size and type.

Parts from different manufacturers will resemble each other, and may even fit other brakes — after a fashion. Parts for other models from the same manufacturer may well fit perfectly; but they will not operate properly. Be sure to state the exact make and model name when ordering.

Brake stirrup arms come in varying lengths. If you are ordering new ones, measure the old ones from the centre of the pivot bolt bushing to the end of the brake shoe adjusting slot, and state this measurement and how you obtained it when placing the order.

As elsewhere, every tiny part and every single washer has its part to play in the proper functioning of the system. Even subtle features of the shape of each part can be important. It pays to know about these, and to visualise how each part operates within the assembly.

Everything begins with the brake arm bridge, or 'horseshoe'; the other parts are all assembled round it. The left spring, for instance, which looks like a toy cannon seen in profile from the right, slips over the left pivot housing that protrudes from the horseshoe; its 'barrel' is then trapped under the stud. Next, the left or outer brake arm is fitted with its two nylon bushings, one from the front and one from the back, and the steel bushing is pushed through. The shoulder of the pivot bolt then passes through the steel bushing, the whole subassembly is moved towards the spring and pivot housing, the bolt end passes through the housing, and is secured by the lock-nut behind the horseshoe.

In theory this leaves one arm of the spring unanchored — but don't panic! All springs must be in tension, and in this case the curving left arm of the spring — the carriage of the toy cannon — is trapped behind a stud on the inner face of the brake arm, or against the lip of the shoe slot. Certainly it will be held in *some* way!

Once the assembly is complete, the spring will always push the arm outwards. Pulling the straddle cable upwards will pivot the arm, forcing the brake shoe against the rim of the wheel, but the moment the operating tension in the brake control linkage is released — in other words, the moment the rider lets go of the brake lever — the pivot spring pushes the brake arm out again.

The main disadvantage of the centre-pull brake is weight, so some machines eliminate the horseshoes. Instead, they have housings and spring

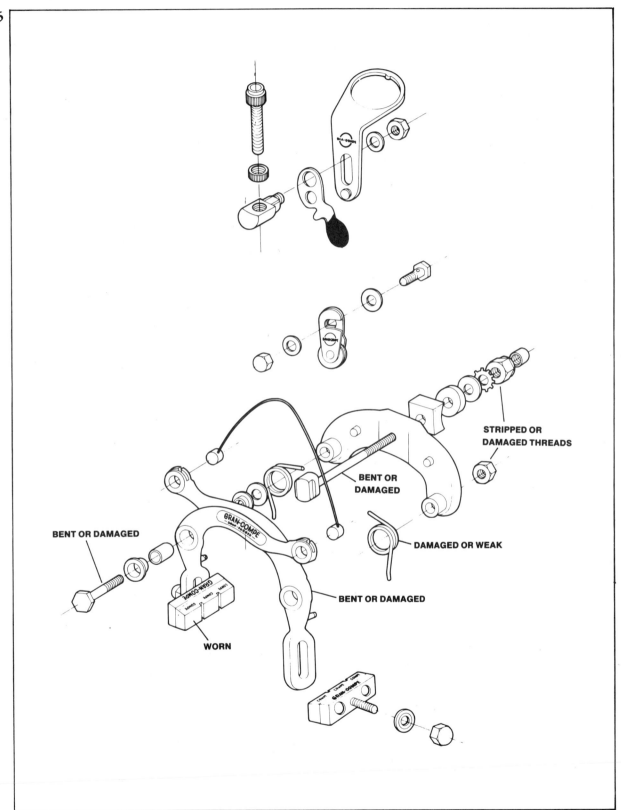

STRIPPED OR
DAMAGED THREADS

BENT OR
DAMAGED

BENT OR DAMAGED

DAMAGED OR WEAK

BENT OR DAMAGED

WORN

97

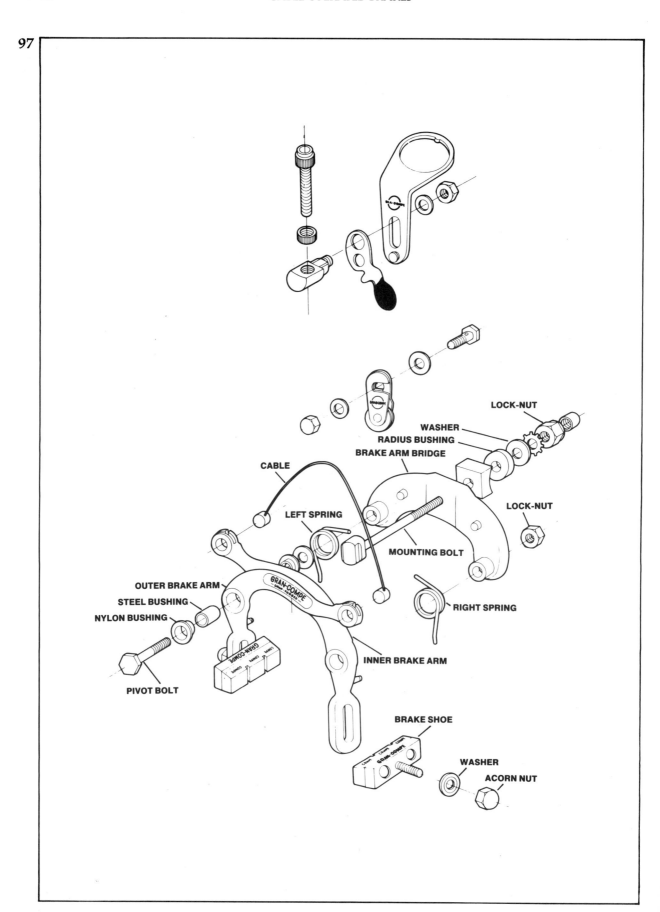

LOCK-NUT

WASHER

RADIUS BUSHING

BRAKE ARM BRIDGE

CABLE

LEFT SPRING

LOCK-NUT

MOUNTING BOLT

OUTER BRAKE ARM

STEEL BUSHING

NYLON BUSHING

RIGHT SPRING

INNER BRAKE ARM

PIVOT BOLT

BRAKE SHOE

WASHER

ACORN NUT

98

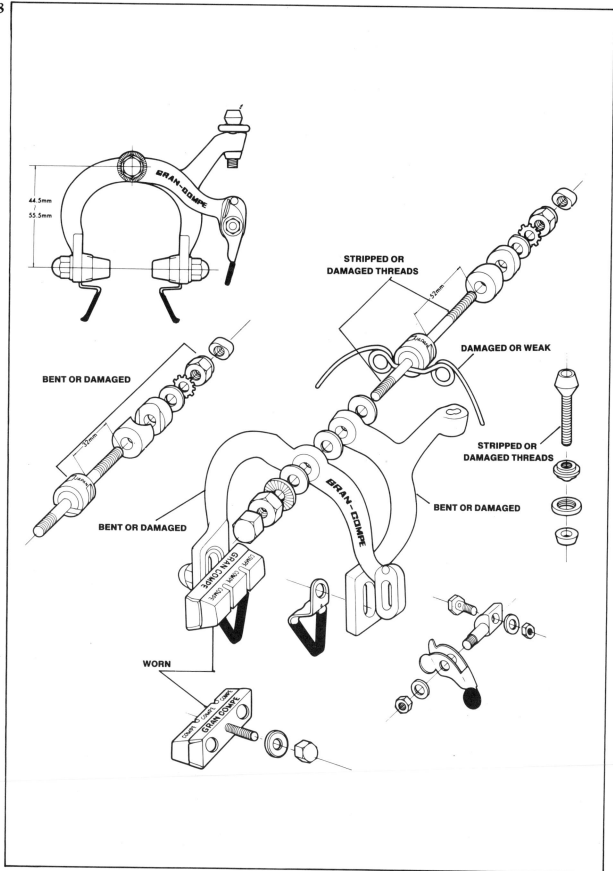

44.5mm
55.5mm

GRAN-COMPE

STRIPPED OR
DAMAGED THREADS

52mm

BENT OR DAMAGED

DAMAGED OR WEAK

32mm

STRIPPED OR
DAMAGED THREADS

BENT OR DAMAGED

GRAN-COMPE

BENT OR DAMAGED

WORN

GRAN COMPE

studs brazed directly to the front fork blades and the seat stays. The brake arm parts are fitted to the housings.

Most tandem bikes have cantilever centre-pulls, in which the straddle cable is attached next to the pivot point. Cantilevers, the most effective centre-pulls, need brazed-on pivot housings.

Side-pull brakes

The only inherent disadvantage of the side-pull brake is that it is not self-adjusting: one arm of the caliper is almost always nearer the wheel rim than the other. But it is a light, simple mechanism, and it needs less mounting hardware for its control cables. High-performance side-pulls (which may cost as much as a complete discount bicycle from a high street chain) will work as well as anyone could wish, even under racing conditions.

Side-pull brakes have a single spring. Its centre section is held in a slot cut across the pivot bolt, and its legs are caught behind lugs on the brake arms. The two loops in the spring simply give it a sturdier, more reliable action.

The spring is the principal maintenance point in the system. Be sure that it is centred across the pivot bolt, and that its two legs fit the same distance into their lugs. The idea is to keep equal tension in the two legs, so that the brake shoes will contact the wheel rim simultaneously, and then retract an equal distance.

In fact, in almost every case one leg of the spring will be stronger, or have a mechanical advantage of some sort over the other. One possible cure is a carefully-delivered blow to the weak side of the spring, using a mallet and an old screwdriver. With the assembly in place, strike down sharply just above the coil. This may reshape the spring to advantage, but often a new spring is the only real solution.

99: Any caliper brake needs to have every part precisely adjusted, especially if it is a side-pull design. Make sure all washers are in place, and all fasteners and lock-nuts on the pivot bolt are adjusted so the various parts can swivel freely but not too loosely. Limit lubrication to a very light touch of dry, non-silicone spray. Replace brake shoes whenever they become worn or hardened; use water as a lubricant when removing or installing them. Be sure that the closed end of the shoe holder faces forward. On women's bicycles, the rear adjuster and anchor will probably have their positions reversed, so the cable may approach from below.

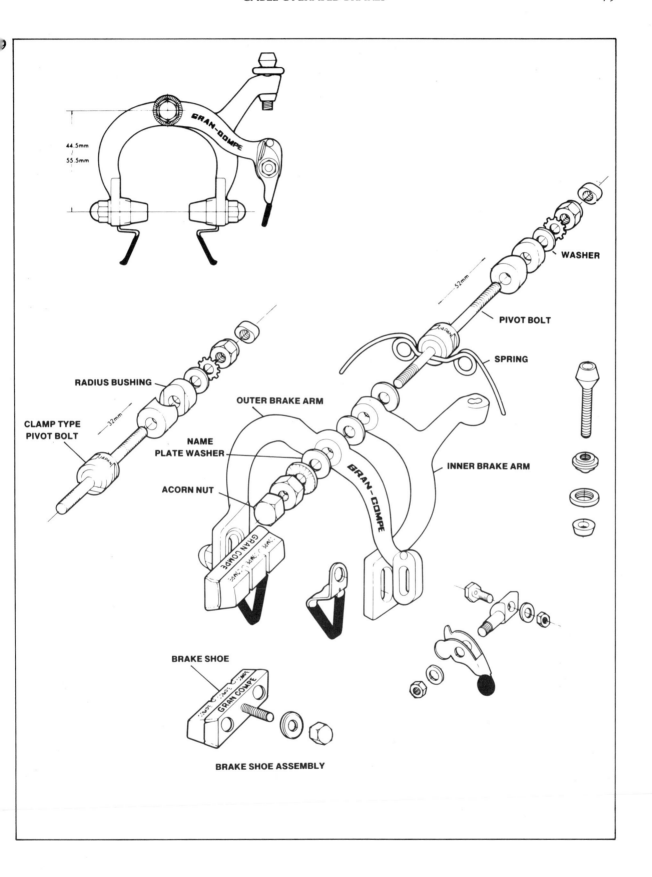

44.5mm
55.5mm

WASHER

52mm

PIVOT BOLT

SPRING

RADIUS BUSHING

OUTER BRAKE ARM

INNER BRAKE ARM

CLAMP TYPE
PIVOT BOLT

NAME
PLATE WASHER

ACORN NUT

BRAKE SHOE

BRAKE SHOE ASSEMBLY

Front and rear derailleurs

The purpose of a derailleur is to move a thin flexible chain from one sprocket to another, assisted to some extent by centrifugal effects. The mechanism is designed to nudge rather than force, and if it meets much resistance it will actually warp temporarily or even permanently.

This is why it is important to keep pedalling while you are changing gear — it helps the chain to jump to the adjacent set of teeth after the derailleur has helped loosen its hold on the original set. It is equally important to plan ahead, and change to a lower gear before the pedal effort becomes too great. Otherwise the system may jam, and then suddenly unjam, if the mechanisms are operated while they are under strain.

Almost all derailleurs use the 'parallelogram principle'; that is, they are boxes that can be made to distort sideways. In practice this means that the front cage (or the rear pulley set) will rise and fall slightly as the chain moves in and out. In front sets this is desirable; in rear sets it is compensated for. Some front derailleurs operate a push-rod angled upwards through a linkage in a sealed box. Some rear derailleurs use a scissors action.

All derailleurs should be kept clean, and lubricated with dry molybdenum spray. When washing a derailleur, make sure you are not washing silt into the various crevices; check the action by hand, feeling for grit.

100: Exploded view of a typical front derailleur; the same unit assembled and seen from the rear is shown in fig. 101. Other units of this general type use rivets instead of pivot bolts. Notice that the traversing spring here has a key at each end; one fits into a hole in the spring housing, the other into a hole in the traversing link. Moving the link is effectively an attempt to wind the coil. The same principle is used at the pulley cages of rear derailleurs. Many front derailleurs push and pull at the spring, but the principle is the same in broad outline. The chain guide cage must be parallel to the chainwheels, and high enough to clear the large chainwheel, yet low enough to guide the chain onto the smaller ones. These adjustments are made at the seat tube clamp. The cage must be properly angled to the curve of the chainwheel, and the front tabs may have to be bent slightly in or out. Minute adjustments like these can be made with the thumb and fingers, or with small tools carefully applied at the cage mounts. Finally, the cage must travel in and out precisely. These adjustments are made at the limit stops, with the machine off the floor, using a vigorous pedalling action to check the results when the operating lever is moved.

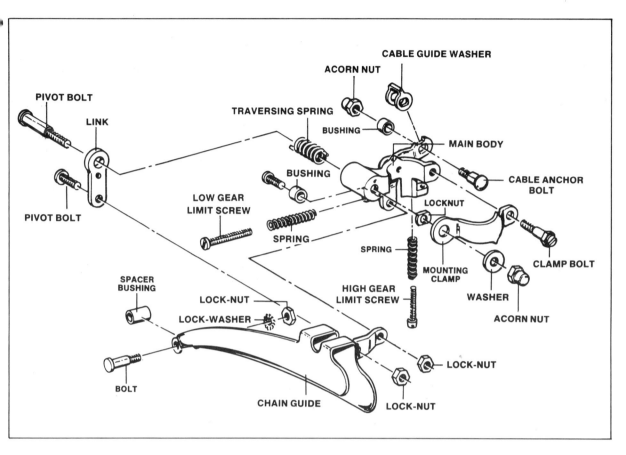

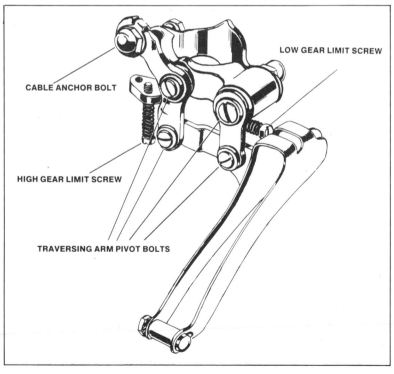

102: The body of this rear derailleur is a folding parallelogram that moves in and out with the chain. It also swings slightly backwards and forwards around its pivot bolt against the spring created by the rear sheath, which ends in a stop on the pivot bolt housing. In addition, the pulley cage rotates against a spring — the system is shown in more detail in fig. 103. Many rear derailleurs are the high-angled 'sidewinder' type, which has more road clearance in a leaning turn. Cages on wide-ratio derailleurs may be much longer than this one, but work on exactly the same principles. Most of the problems with derailleurs arise from adjustment difficulties; the rest are usually the result of stiff pivots and weak or broken springs.

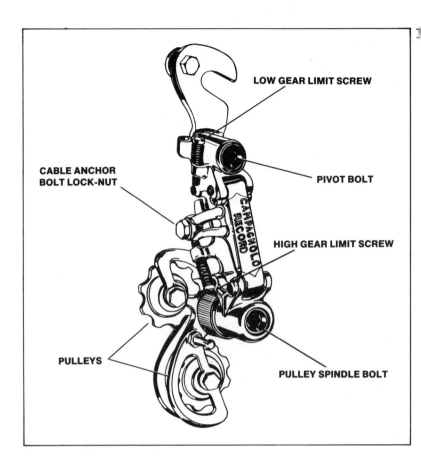

Rebuilding derailleurs

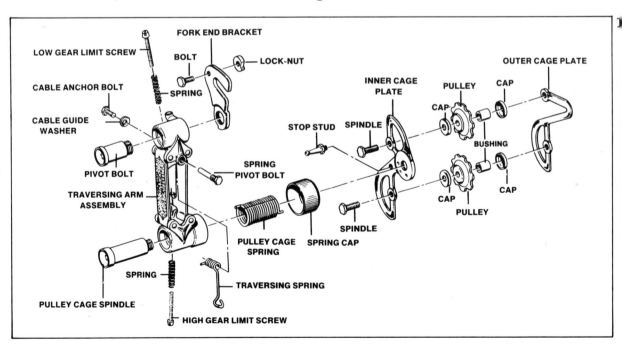

4

104: The pulleys must be exactly parallel to the sprockets. If the rear wheel is correctly positioned and the freewheel block is properly seated on the hub threads, but the pulleys are out of line in the horizontal or vertical planes, then the derailleur body is out of true. Check the pivot bolt mountings. If those are straight, then the derailleur can be bent back into position — but be careful!

103: An exploded view of the Campagnolo 'Record' derailleur, made of plated brass. The 'Nuovo Record' is similar, but made of alloy. Both use plastic pulleys with sleeve-bearing bushes. The earlier 'Gran Sport' has a brass body and steel pulleys with spindle cones and very small ball bearings. The spindle bolts for all three will fit the other models, but must not be interchanged freely; various sub-models of these models use shoulder bolts as spindles, and threaded bolts will create a mysterious squeak while you are riding. Such small variations, with their attendant problems for the hasty mechanic, are typical of derailleurs, especially rear derailleurs. Notice the fork-end bracket. Some machines provide housings at the right fork-end, where the pivot screws in directly. Be sure the housing is tapped for the size of pivot bolt you are using.

106

CHAIN ON SECOND SPROCKET

HIGH GEAR LIMIT SCREW
LOW GEAR LIMIT SCREW

105: The pulleys must rotate to take slack out of the chain as it moves down from the larger sprockets. On most derailleurs, there are several choices of tension. If the pulley hangs limp, the spring must be broken or out of its key; when servicing, note the order and orientation of its washers very carefully. Check for rust as a cause of stiffness.

106: Adjust the high gear limit screw (to the right on this SunTour model) with the chain on the second sprocket. In use, the system will take enough pressure from the chain line to drop the chain onto the first, smallest, sprocket. Set the low gear limit screw (on the left) with the same principle in mind. There is so much power in low gear that the cage can be forced into the spokes if you forget.

107: Variations in tooth count from cluster to cluster (see page 90) are taken care of by the cage pivot spring. Machines with extremely low gears need longer pulley cages. But if a pulley wraps round almost to a horizontal position in top gear, the chain is probably too long. If it grinds against the wider sprockets, the chain is probably too short.

108

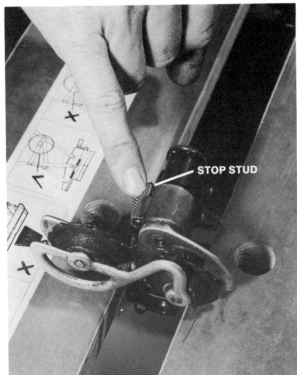

10

108: This sequence shows you how to take apart the most frequently serviced part of a rear derailleur (aside from the pulleys, which need periodic cleaning and light greasing at the bearings). Hold the cage firmly while removing the stop stud with a small spanner.

109: Some derailleurs, such as the Campagnolo Super Record, have a stop screw that can be undone a few turns.

1

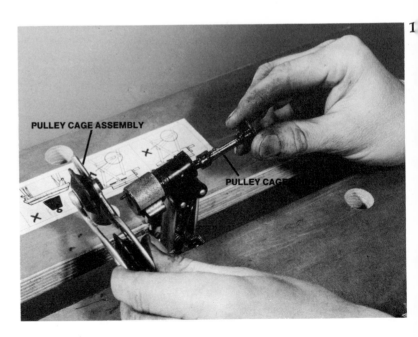

110: Now let the cage unwind. Take out the spindle bolt, and pull the cage assembly away. With a hook-spring derailleur, you will be close to this point simply by unhooking the spring.

SPRING CAP   **PULLEY CAGE SPRING**

TRAVERSING ARM ASSEMBLY

PIVOT BOLT

111: Now remove the spring cap, carefully take out the spring, and note the position of all washers and keys. Check, and replace anything that is worn, stiff or rusty. Lightly grease new parts as you fit them. Wind up the cage again before you refit the stud.

112: The body leaves its mount when the pivot bolt is removed, and the traversing spring can be taken off in a similar way. That leaves a light metal box with rivets at the four corners. Tight or loose rivets can be repaired by prising at the box carefully with a thin-bladed screwdriver, or by tapping the rivet heads with a blunt punch. But if there is a problem it was probably caused by an accidental blow which is also likely to have warped the body. You can prise and tap plated derailleurs back into shape if you work carefully. Avoid straining the rivets; replace them if you can obtain new ones. Alloy derailleurs will bend up to a point, then snap just like dry cheddar cheese.

Rear-wheel assemblies

Rear-wheel assemblies for derailleurs are made up of essentially familiar parts, but deserve closer examination before we take a look at the freewheel block. A great deal is happening here, and repair or maintenance work that fails to take all of it into account may do more harm than good in the long run.

The freewheel block may seem simple; in fact it is a complete subject in itself, and is discussed in detail in the next section. For the moment, it should be enough to remind you that the hub mounting threads on the body of the freewheel block are hard, sharp and fine — but the matching threads on the alloy hub are fine, only initially sharp, and *soft*. Every time a freewheel is screwed on or off, even if the job is done carefully using a freewheel that fits the hub, some damage is done. If you work very carefully, the damage will remain within reasonable limits. It usually does. But remember: every time you fit a freewheel block you could destroy a hub shell with a single twist of the wrist.

Any break in the spokes on the right-hand side will require you to take off the freewheel block before you can replace the spoke. Careful wheel maintenance and good riding habits will soon bring their own reward! So will a careful setting of the low gear limit on the derailleur. If you ride without a spoke disc, the only thing that can save your spokes is good gear changing. Even with a disc, bad gear changing can scrape the derailleur and damage the disc.

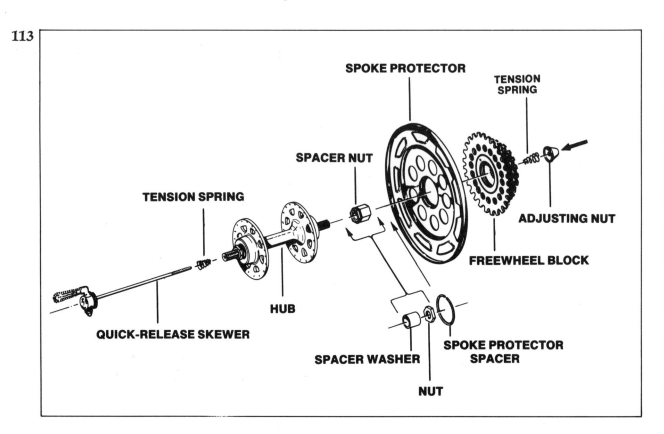

113

SPOKE PROTECTOR

TENSION SPRING

SPACER NUT

TENSION SPRING

ADJUSTING NUT

FREEWHEEL BLOCK

HUB

QUICK-RELEASE SKEWER

SPACER WASHER

SPOKE PROTECTOR SPACER

NUT

Your choice of threaded or unthreaded axle spacers will depend on the exact depth of the freewheel block and the fit of your removing tool. It may be more convenient to have a spacer that will fall off, rather than one that will need to be worked off at a point where there is little margin for movement.

The hollow axle used for quick-release hubs bends a little more readily than the solid ones do.

A quick-release mechanism should be set once, for the correct pressure — after that you should try to leave the adjusting nut alone. The mechanism should not impose a crushing grip on the fork-ends; you should be able to close it with about as much force as you would use on the catch of a suitcase. If you have taken it apart for some reason, make sure that the tension springs are pointing inwards. Crushed springs should be replaced. Put a little white grease on the cam inside the lever housing. (If you unfasten the acorn nut or C-clip it will all slip apart in your hands.)

Freewheel blocks

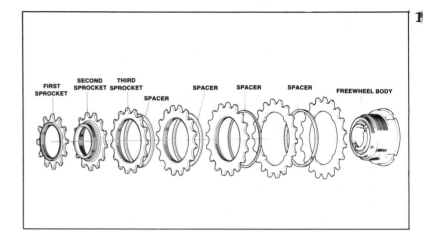

The single most important development of bicycle technology is the multiple freewheel or 'block'. With it, bicycles can move up any gradient, or against any wind, at the best possile speed and in some degree of comfort. Today, freewheel blocks normally have five, six or even seven sprockets, all of which can be chosen from a wide variety of sizes to suit the particular needs of individual riders. With a selection of different chainwheel sizes it is possible to build up a ten-, twelve-, fifteen- or even twenty-one-speed machine that will allow the rider to cross the Alps without ever having to stand up on the pedals. Ten speeds (or even seven or eight significant differences in gear ratio) will do for any normal purpose, however.

At the heart of all this is the freewheel body, which is essentially a ratcheting mechanism. The inner body, which threads to the hub, is stationary. The outer shell is threaded or splined to accommodate the sprockets, and rotates around the inner body on small ball bearings. One of these two principal parts is notched. The other, usually the inner body, bears matching pawls. These little sprung teeth, looking rather like the heads of water birds, duck down and click into the notches when the outer shell coasts or is turned backwards, but lift their beaks and engage firmly in the notches when the action of the chain on the sprockets pulls the shell forward. This transmits rotation to the hub shell.

The typical freewheel body is keyed, and can be opened by unscrewing. But body repair is really more of a pastime than a practical remedy. When the pawls break, or become irretrievably clogged with dirty oil, the only real solution is to buy a new unit. If you still feel like trying it, I suggest strong light, quiet surroundings, time, and — rarest of all — a reliable source of new parts. Everything inside is critical, even the built-in wobble that allows the sprockets to make slight adjustments to changing chain-line angles.

The block shown in fig. 114 is typical. It can be removed by unscrewing the stationary body with a splined tool.

In the Atom design, the fourth and fifth sprockets have left-hand threads. Many Japanese designs use splined sprockets that slip off after the first or second sprocket has been unscrewed.

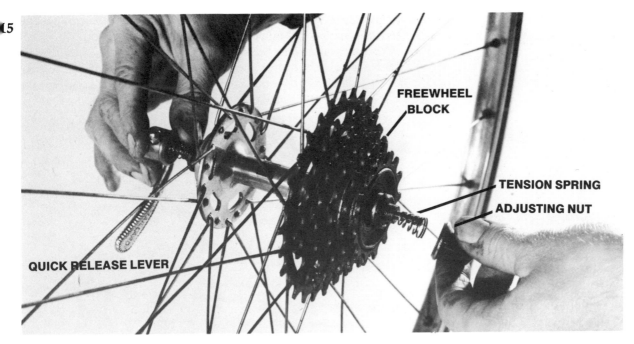

15

FREEWHEEL
BLOCK

TENSION SPRING

ADJUSTING NUT

QUICK RELEASE LEVER

16

115: To remove a freewheel block, begin by removing the axle fastener on the freewheel side. If the wheel is fitted with quick-release, like this one, take off the adjusting nut and both tension springs. Now test the fit of the extractor tool in the splines or keyways of the freewheel body.

116: Remove any washers and spacers that prevent the tool from seating completely on the freewheel body. A perfect fit is vital, or the body keys will be damaged — in extreme cases, this will prevent the freewheel from being removed from the hub. If the body shows signs of earlier damage, a tightly-fitting tool is the only hope.

Alloy sprockets are available for racers. Most other riders will find durable steel sprockets perfectly satisfactory.

You can make a sprocket-removing tool at home, using loops of old derailleur chain passed through short lengths of pipe. Make a small loop at the other end of the pipe or the handle, and retain it with a nut and bolt. For the home mechanic, professional tools are rarely worth the money.

All freewheel bodies *appear* to be 35mm threaded; only Italian ones actually are. French models, although they, too, are metric, are really a few micrometres smaller. English bodies are very close in size, but are measured in decimal parts of an inch. Any mechanic who feels so inclined can thread any given block onto any given hub, but if they are from different countries then the combination will probably serve to strip the threads.

When installing a sprocket, grease the threads lightly — and take it easy. Seat the sprocket by hand; riding the machine in low gear will move it the last few millimetres up the threads. (Do *not* stand on the pedals, and be ready for the sprocket to move slightly inward towards the spokes.)

11

117: Now fasten the tool in place, using the unsprung quick-release or conventional axle fasteners. A very small amount of slack — no more than a hair — should be left in the fastening, so that the tool can back up enough to start the unthreading. This example is a universal tool that fits many blocks. Like all other tools, it can be used by gripping it with a spanner while holding the wheel upright in the other hand. Press down on the inflated tyre from the top, and push the spanner decisively.

11

118: Another method is to clamp the tool in a vice. Grasp the wheel at the rim and turn it. The fastener must now be unscrewed a little, and the wheel turned again; then the whole process must be repeated. This is an excellent way to move a stubborn block but a clumsy way to finish the job. Remember to turn the wheel anticlockwise. When the block is off, soak and wash it thoroughly in solvent, spinning it and flushing it as carefully as possible. Let it dry and test it for grittiness. If necessary, wash it again. When you are satisfied, pump light oil between the body and the shell, turning it, until the pawls begin to cluck rather than click, and excess oil is dripping out on the other side of the body. Spin the block and continue to wipe it clean for a while, then set it down on a paper towel and let it drain overnight. Add a few drops of oil in the morning, and replace the block.

FREEWHEEL VICE INSERT

SPROCKET TOOL

119: To take a block apart, unthread the first sprocket while holding the others firm in a freewheel vice insert. Once the first threaded element has been removed, the rest may lift off — if not, check thread direction and continue.

120: On this SunTour block, a second sprocket is unscrewed. Then the rest of the spacers and sprockets simply lift away from the splined body.

SECOND SPROCKET

121: When replacing sprockets, be sure that they are flat, and that the spline or thread is properly engaged. Notice that the first sprocket here threads to the second sprocket, not to the freewheel body itself.

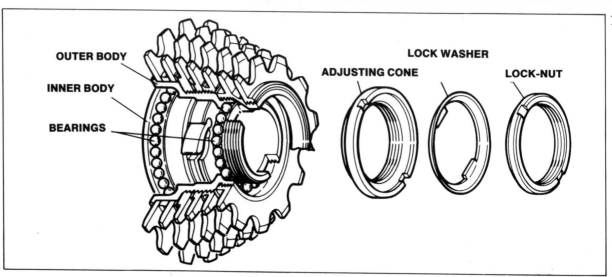

OUTER BODY

INNER BODY

BEARINGS

LOCK WASHER

ADJUSTING CONE

LOCK-NUT

Developing your skills

As time passes and your experience grows you will find your attitudes towards bicycle repair beginning to change. To begin with you will probably feel that something awful has just happened, or is about to happen, and there will be nothing you can do about it. But by degrees, you will acquire the same practised confidence as the mechanic in your local bicycle shop.

As you begin your very first repair job, you are already starting a mental file of useful short-cuts, and of errors to avoid. Gradually you will gather a useful armoury of special tools that suit your particular working methods. Any old bolt or broken screwdriver can be used as a punch, but after a while you will find one or two that you like to keep close to hand. A particular piece of dowelling will be just the right length for punching out the headset cups on family bicycles. You will know precisely the right place to set up the repair stand, or the workbench corner on which the bike is hung, so as to avoid torn clothes or a bruised elbow.

Saving the pieces

Before long you will also gather a collection of jam-jars, shoeboxes, shelves, and eventually professional cabinets, full of salvaged nuts and bolts, cotter pins, potentially useful bearings, odd pedals, slightly damaged luggage carriers, cracked reflectors, and odds and ends of handlebar tape. And when it all begins to get on top of you, you can always hand out some of the less immediately useful bits and pieces to the younger amateur mechanics in your area!

Of course, this proliferation only happens if you allow your original interest in solving a specific problem, or maintaining a particular machine, to grow into a hobby that makes you the family shop and the neighbourhood expert. This is a road that could very well lead you to a garage full of salvaged frames and parts. From these you will be perfectly capable of building abused-looking but perfectly serviceable machines for riding to school or into town. Even so, the number of parts available will soon become ridiculously large, and before long you will grow ruthlessly selective. Like the professional mechanic, you will never save bearings, you will keep a small supply of new washers and throw away any that are old or bent, and you will never think twice about replacing an old cotter pin. When in doubt, throw it out.

Confidence

Many mechanics pass through a stage where they will turn their hand to anything, converting three-speeds into ten-speeds, and putting together brake assemblies from parts supplied by three different manufacturers. It is a stage that will yield its own accomplishments and its own lessons, and for that reason alone is not to be despised. But eventually it becomes more trouble than it is really worth. It has served its purpose in showing that anything is possible with the help of a little common sense — and it has laid a foundation of advanced experience.

Engineering and physics

It is perfectly possible to service and repair an assembly without ever looking at a diagram. Once the pieces are in your hand, it is easy enough to see broken metal, or work out how to insert a replacement part.

But the best kind of mechanical thinking comes from an understanding of the behaviour of systems in action. The engineers who designed those parts took many things into account: the effects of centrifugal force on rotating assemblies, of dirtied oil channels on the cooling of a part, of the way in which two parts squeeze together in tight places, or of heat on the structure of a metal, which might cause an apparently sound part to shatter or bend. No part is superfluous, and few of its features are liable to be simply decorative. The bicycle is a machine — and it's worth remembering that this machine gave birth to the aeroplane.

Learning to use skills effectively

Only experience can teach you to make the best possible use of your skills, and so increase your enjoyment. Doing a difficult job well is always satisfying — doing it efficiently and quickly can only add to that satisfaction. As your knowledge grows you will be able to tackle larger, more ambitious projects. Your early experience will have taught you what is possible — and eventually you will be able to put together a custom-built machine that meets your own precise requirements, or a road bike that is exactly right for the area where you live. Work at this level could become very profitable — and for those who need something more substantial to look forward to than the sheer pleasure of it all, this may be the incentive you need to take those first, awkward and often frustrating steps on the road to a fully-developed skill.